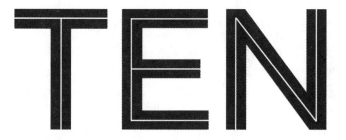

# TEN

*how the commandments*

## SET US FREE

# mark mitchell

## Discovery House®
from Our Daily Bread Ministries

*In honor of my parents, Dr. Stewart and Jean Mitchell.*
*"Like arrows in the hands of a warrior are children born in one's youth"*
*(Psalm 127:4).*

*Ten: How the Commandments Set Us Free*

© 2016 by Mark Mitchell

Discovery House is affiliated with Our Daily Bread Ministries, Grand Rapids, Michigan.

Requests for permission to quote from this book should be directed to: Permissions Department, Discovery House, P.O. Box 3566, Grand Rapids, MI 49501, or contact us by e-mail at permissionsdept@dhp.org.

All Scripture quotations, unless otherwise indicated, are taken from the Holy Bible, New International Version®, NIV®. Copyright © 1973, 1978, 1984, 2011 by Biblica, Inc.™ Used by permission of Zondervan. All rights reserved worldwide. www.zondervan.com. The "NIV" and "New International Version" are trademarks registered in the United States Patent and Trademark Office by Biblica, Inc.™

*Interior design by* Michelle Espinoza

**Library of Congress Cataloging-in-Publication Data**
Mitchell, Mark, 1956- author.
Ten: how the commandments set us free / Mark Mitchell.
  p. cm.
Includes bibliographical references.
  ISBN 978-1-62707-486-5
1. Ten commandments. I. Title.
  BV4655. M45 2016
  241.5'2—dc23                                              2015030861

Printed in the United States of America
Second printing in 2016

# CONTENTS

# INTRODUCTION

Everyone knows the Ten Commandments, right? Well, sort of. Unfortunately, as our society has drifted from its biblical moorings, there's been more and more confusion and outright ignorance about the Ten Commandments. One study found that Americans are more familiar with the ingredients of a McDonald's Big Mac hamburger than some of the Ten Commandments. Eighty percent of respondents knew that a Big Mac contains "two all-beef patties," but only six out of ten could identify "Thou shalt not kill" as one of the Ten Commandments. Also, while 43 percent of respondents (including those who are regular church-goers) could name the least familiar members of the *Brady Bunch* TV family (Bobby and Peter), fewer people could recall the two least familiar commandments— "Remember the Sabbath" (34 percent) and "Do not make any false idols" (29 percent).

Of course, you probably know at least *something* about the Ten Commandments—like the fact that there are ten of them. And you might even be able to list at least a few of them. But did you know that the entire list actually appears twice in the Bible? Exodus 20 tells how they were originally given to Moses on Mount Sinai. Then in Deuteronomy 5 Moses repeats them for the Israelites before they enter the Promised Land.

This book devotes one chapter to each of the Ten Commandments, taking a closer look at them one at a time and then applying each of them to our lives.

In reality, many people—even followers of Jesus—have a negative view of these commandments. For me as I was growing up, the Ten Commandments had flashing red lights all over them, warning me that if I've trespassed even one, I was going straight to hell. Most of us don't enjoy lists that start with "Thou shalt not."

But God didn't give these commandments to enslave us. They were provided to enrich us. The Ten Commandments are meant to be a green light—a green light to freedom. Imagine being in a strange place and trying to get somewhere without any directions. You'd be totally lost. You'd be frustrated and miserable. You'd get nowhere. The Ten Commandments are simple, clear directions about how to safely get from here to there in life.

But there is more. Most of us believe in God. But do we know what He is like? Do we know what He wants? With the Ten Commandments, we don't have to guess any longer.

You might be thinking, *What if I read the Ten Commandments and just get a massive dose of guilt because I've already violated many of them?* It's important to understand the Ten Commandments in relation to the rest of the Bible. In the flow of the biblical story, they weren't given as a requirement for salvation; they were given as a response to the salvation God already provided as a free gift. That's why the Ten Commandments begin with these words: "I am the Lord your God who brought you out of Egypt, out of the land of slavery." In other words, God is saying: "Even before I gave you these laws, I delivered you and made you My people. I'm not giving you these commandments so you can earn that privilege. I'm giving them to you because I love you, I'm committed to you, and I want you to experience freedom. I didn't bring you out of slavery to put you under a whole new kind of slavery."

The Ten Commandments always need to be placed right beside the gospel. The gospel tells us that Jesus came to bring us out of our own Egypt—to save us from our slavery to sin. He did what we couldn't do. He lived the sinless life we couldn't live, and He died to free us. We don't earn that; we just receive it by faith.

So now, as grateful children, we don't ignore God's law and then live in guilt; rather, we gladly embrace it. We want to please the One who rescued us. Yet we're still like toddlers learning to walk. We stumble a lot, and at times the law does remind us of the areas where we fall. The law is like a mirror that shows us the dirt on our faces, but when that happens we're not meant to wallow in guilt—we're meant to turn back to Christ for cleansing. (See 1 John 1:9.) The Ten Commandments show us the way to live while continually pointing us back to our need for a Savior—our need for Jesus Christ—the One who can set us free.

# 1

# RECOGNIZING THE
# ONE CENTER

The first commandment seems pretty straightforward: "I am the LORD your God, who brought you out of Egypt, out of the land of slavery. You shall have no other gods before me" (Exodus 20:2–3). Unfortunately, it is easy to misunderstand this commandment. Sometimes we use it to wag our finger at "those people" who worship other gods. But God isn't saying anything here about other people and their gods; he's speaking to His own people about His role in their lives. Nor is this saying that somehow God is needy for our attention. He's not some kind of insecure prima donna who can't share the stage. He doesn't need our worship. He desires it.

This commandment also doesn't mean that God should become our "top priority." Often, Christians will have a list of priorities with God at the top, the family second, and job or something else third. That kind of thinking assumes we can divide our lives into clean and tidy boxes—a God box, a family box, and a job box. On Sunday we open the God box, at home we open the family box, and at work we open the job box. There is little or no integration; we often live by one set of values at church, another at home, and still another at work. That's not what God had in mind when He gave the first commandment.

## THE ONE AT THE CENTER

Instead, through the first commandment God is saying, "I don't want to just be number one on your list. I want to be the One at the center of it all. I want to be the hub of the wheel that holds every spoke of your life together. I want to be your ultimate concern. I want to be your singular passion. I don't want anything to rival the place I have in your life. There can be nothing in your life that compares with me." The sixteenth-century reformer John Calvin said this kind of ordering really boils down to four things: *adoration, trust, invocation*, and *thanksgiving*.

*God desires our adoration.* God wants to be the One who captures your attention, the One you cannot get enough of, and the One you love to talk about.

*God desires our trust.* God wants to be the One you depend on for everything, the One who gives you a deep sense of security because you know you can count on Him for everything—from your eternal salvation to your daily bread.

*God desires our invocation.* God wants to be the One you turn to in times of need, the One you run to when you're in trouble.

When you need forgiveness, wisdom, or encouragement, He wants you to turn to Him.

*God desires our thanksgiving.* God wants to be the One you thank when your table is full—when your heart overflows with an abundance of hope and joy.

## ROOM FOR ONLY ONE THRONE

Why should God occupy this place in our life?

First, He deserves it. Notice the first four words in verse 2: "I am the LORD." Don't pass over that. That's a statement about who God is. When God appeared to Moses in the burning bush and Moses asked God what his name was, God answered with this statement: "I AM WHO I AM" (Exodus 3:14). In other words, "I am the sovereign ruler of the universe. I made it all. I sustain it all. I control it all. I'm not limited by time. I AM."

At that time Egypt was the world power, and the pharaoh was viewed as an all-powerful god. But then Yahweh came along and said, "Let me show you who is really in charge." When God sent the ten plagues, when He opened up the Red Sea and let the Israelites pass through, when the Israelites made it safely through and the waters came down and drowned Pharaoh's army, God demonstrated His power.

God is not only sovereign but He's also *personal.* That's why He says, "I am the LORD your God" (Exodus 20:2). When He says, "your God," He's talking to you and me on a personal basis. He's not a God who exists way out there in the recesses of the universe and has no time for or interest in you. He's not a distant, unapproachable king. He's a personal God. He knows you, and He wants to be known by you.

Second, God should be hub of our lives, because if He is, that will determine everything else about us. Everything gets aligned or misaligned from that hub. It's like buttoning the wrong button at the top of your shirt: each of the other buttons is subsequently thrown off. If we don't get this first commandment right, the rest of our life gets out of whack. Everything flows out of this commandment.

The Ten Commandments start with the vertical; they start with our relationship with God. Only after we get that right can we turn to the horizontal—our relationship with other people. Some people want to preserve the second section of the commandments (starting with "Honor your father and mother") but ignore the first section (the first four commandments, which deal with our relationship with God). They may agree that murder, adultery, stealing, and lying are wrong, but they want this moral code without the God who himself defines morality. In reality, however, if you cut out the author of life, it's hard to respect life. If you cut out the author of marriage, it's hard to respect the marriage vows. If you cut out the author of truth, it's hard to tell the truth.

Third, God wants to occupy this place in our lives because

there's room for only one throne in our hearts. The story in the gospels about the "rich young ruler" (Luke 18:18, Matthew 19:22) illustrates this point. He approached Jesus and asked what he needed to do to inherit eternal life. Jesus told him to keep the commandments. The young man made the startling claim that he had been keeping them his whole life. Jesus put that claim to the test. "One thing you lack," [Jesus] said. "Go, sell everything you have and give to the poor, and you will have treasure in heaven. Then come, follow me" (Mark 10:21). The young man had nothing to say to that, and he walked away sad. Jesus had just exposed his real god. At that moment the rich young man realized he hadn't kept all the commandments; he hadn't even gotten past the first one. He had put his money before God. As Oswald Chambers once wrote, "If I enthrone anything other than God in my life, God retires and lets the other god do what it can."

## IDOLS OF THE HEART

We know that God is supposed to be the hub of our lives, but we all struggle with a subtle (or not-so-subtle) drift toward other gods. This doesn't mean that we worship little idols made out of wood or stone. Most of us don't have a golden calf stationed in our backyard that we worship during every full moon. But we have plenty of "idols of the heart." John Calvin called these "shadow deities." These are most often good things given to us by God, but somehow, because of our own twisted nature, we take these good gifts and give them more significance than we should.

We were created with certain needs: security, significance, purpose. Throughout our lives we discover that some of these needs can be at least partially met by the good gifts of creation. It might be a particular talent that gives us a sense of identity or purpose. It might be a hobby, like scuba diving or hunting or participating in triathlons. It might be material things like food or wine or furniture or cars. It might even be something as wonderful and God-given as our marriage, our children, or our friends. These good things easily become idols when we move them into the center of our lives. But there's one simple question that can expose these heart idols: *How do I react when someone or something threatens to take them from me?* If a good thing in your life is threatened, you'll most likely struggle and grieve deeply. But if an "ultimate thing" is threatened, your life unravels; you may even descend into despair.

In this sense, I can't help but think of Abraham. Abraham and Sarah had waited their whole lives for a son. Finally, when it seemed to be too late and they had given up hope, God gave them Isaac. So it was certainly strange when God told Abraham to sacrifice his own son on the altar—not a metaphorical altar, mind you, but a real one with a real knife. We wonder what kind of God would ask for that from a father. It's even more shocking to see Abraham climbing up Mount Moriah ready to do the unthinkable. What kind of father is he? It was obviously difficult for Abraham. But the root question of this story has to do with the first commandment: Did Abraham have any gods before Yahweh? Had he taken this gift from God and given his son ultimate significance in his life? No.

God stopped Abraham from killing Isaac, but Abraham passed the test that the rich young man of Mark 10 would later fail.

One of the ways we know if a good thing has become an idol is by the impact it has on our lives. When good gifts become idols, they tend to spoil—they tend to become burdensome compulsions. That's one of the major themes in the classic movie *Chariots of Fire*, the story of two real-life Olympic runners. Eric Liddell is a Christian, and Harold Abrahams is a secular Jew. Both run for Great Britain, but Abrahams runs for his own glory and is so afraid of losing that he can't even take pleasure in winning. Running has become a compulsion, not a joy. Liddell, on the other hand, puts his call to serve and obey God first in his life. He shows his willingness to put God at the center of his life by refusing to run on Sunday. Yet, in contrast to Abrahams, Liddell actually runs with joy. At one point in the film he says, "God made me fast. When I run, I feel His pleasure." When good things have their proper place in our lives, they bring us pleasure rather than pain.

## EVALUATE YOUR LIFE

Occasionally, it's important to step back from our lives and evaluate whether or not God is our true hub. Is He really first—not in the sense that there are other things on our list but in the sense that He's the center of our existence? Someone made an acrostic out of the word "first" that might help us evaluate our own lives according to the first commandment.

*Focus.* What is your focus? What do you think about? What are you watching? What are you listening to? In Colossians Paul says to "set your minds on things above, not on earthly things" (Colossians 3:2).

*Income.* How do you spend your money? We tend to pour our dollars into things that are meaningful to us. Jesus put it this way: "For where your treasure is, there your heart will be also" (Matthew 6:21). If someone were to evaluate what's important to you based on your checkbook register or your online bank statement, what would that person conclude?

*Relationships.* Who influences your life? Who is in your inner circle? Who do you go to when you need some counsel? Perhaps even a better question is this: Who are you trying to please? Or this: Who are you trying to impress?

*Spiritual food.* How is your spiritual diet? What place does the Word of God really have in your life? Are you feasting on the Word of God on a regular basis? The apostle Peter said, "Like newborn babies, crave pure spiritual milk" (1 Peter 2:2). Does that describe you?

***Time.*** How do you spend your time? We all need time for important relationships, time for work, and time for play. It's amazing, though, how many hours we can spend doing things that really aren't that necessary or important. Then, when it comes to the things of God, we say, "I don't have time for that." Scripture says, "Be very careful, then, how you live—not as unwise but as wise, making the most of every opportunity, because the days are evil" (Ephesians 5:15–16).

## THE PATH TO FREEDOM

When I ask myself these questions, I quickly realize how often I fall short. Here's my prescription: Simply run to Jesus. Instead of feeling guilty and burdened by your sin, confess your sin and remember God's promise in Romans 8:1: "There is now no condemnation for those who are in Christ Jesus."

But don't stop there. Take the next step and ask God to help you make some changes. If you know Christ, then the Holy Spirit lives within you, and the Holy Spirit doesn't just convict you from the outside, He also helps and empowers you from the inside. Remember, the Ten Commandments are meant to enrich you, not to enslave you. You can yield to the Holy Spirit and begin to make God your only God. That's the path to true freedom.

# 2

# DETECTING SUBTLE IDOLS

The first commandment tells us not to worship false gods, and the second says, "You shall not make for yourself an idol" (Exodus 20:4 NASB). These two sound almost the same. But the second commandment isn't concerned with false gods; rather, it's concerned with worshiping the true God falsely. The first commandment is about who or what we worship; the second commandment is about how we worship. The first commandment is about worshiping the right God; the second commandment is about worshiping the right God in the right way.

Here's a real-life example. A twenty-four-year-old man named Dave Davila took a job in Chicago and had to leave his close-knit family. His mother missed him so much that she took a digital photo of him and had it blown up to his actual height and mounted on heavy cardboard. In this way, they actually had "Dave" standing around, hands in his pockets, dressed in his favorite blue button-down shirt hanging untucked over his khaki shorts. They called him "Flat Dave." At first, Flat Dave just stood quietly by at family gatherings. Then word spread throughout the town, and he became a celebrity. Complete strangers wanted to pose with him. His brother said, "I think Flat Dave's actually better looking." Things got somewhat awkward for the real Dave, who his family began calling "Thick Dave." He said, "I'm in Chicago talking to my mom on the phone, and she says, 'Hold on, I've got to load you into the van.' It's a little weird."

The problem isn't that his family has replaced Dave with another son. The problem is that they're trying to stay close to Dave through an image of him. This is exactly what the Israelites did when they got impatient while Moses was on Mount Sinai. They told Aaron to make them a god they could see and touch, so Aaron melted down their jewelry and made a golden calf. But listen to what he said: "These are your gods, Israel, who brought you up out of Egypt" (Exodus 32:4). In effect, Aaron was saying that this was the same God as before; the only difference was that the people now had an image of Him. Something they could see and touch had replaced the real God.

## THE LIKENESS ISN'T THE REAL THING

Simply put, the second commandment means that we're not to use man-made representations of God for the purposes of worship. That's why the second commandment goes on to say, "You shall not make for yourself an image in the form of anything in heaven above or on the earth beneath or in the waters below. You shall not bow down to them or worship them" (Exodus 20:4–5). The Israelites had been living with the Egyptians, who worshiped many gods, most of which they represented in the form of animals. For example, the god Horus had the head of a falcon; the god Anubis had the form of a jackal. The Egyptians bowed down to these images. But God didn't want the Israelites to use any likeness of Him when they worshiped Him.

This doesn't mean religious art is somehow inappropriate. One of my favorite books is *My Name Is Asher Lev* by Chaim Potok. It's about a boy who is a gifted artist, a prodigy, who grows up as a Hasidic Jew. Hasidic Jews don't allow art of any kind, in fear of breaking the second commandment. But the point of the second commandment is not that God is opposed to art.

When it was time to build the tabernacle, the Spirit of God inspired certain Israelites to "make artistic designs for work in gold, silver and bronze, to cut and set stones, to work in wood, and to engage in all kinds of crafts" (Exodus 31:4–5). It's not wrong to create art, and it doesn't mean that artistic symbols are wrong. All the art in the tabernacle was symbolic, and we have a symbol in the cross. In addition, Jesus gave us a very powerful symbol in the bread and the cup of communion. We don't worship those symbols, but we do use them in worship.

The second commandment forbids creating images of God that become objects of worship. There is a fine line here. Symbols are one thing, but to somehow try to replicate the very image of God, whether in a painting or a statue, crosses a line into false worship. In the dome of the Sistine Chapel, Michelangelo's depiction of God reaching out and touching Adam is a beautiful work of art. And it's as natural and good to appreciate that as we would a spectacular sunset. But if somehow that imagined likeness of God becomes the reality of God in your worship, then something is wrong.

You might wonder, *Why did this commandment make the top ten? What harm is there in using images if they help me get closer to God and worship Him? What could be so wrong with that?* Let me give you a few reasons.

## EVERY LIKENESS FALLS SHORT

Man-made images of God inevitability distort the glory of God. As John Calvin wrote:

> A true image of God is not to be found in all the world; and hence . . . His glory is defiled, and His truth corrupted by the lie, whenever He is set before our eyes in a visible form. . . . Therefore to devise any image of God is itself impious, because by this corruption His majesty is adulterated and He is figured to be other than He is.[1]

The Israelites thought there would be no harm in creating a likeness of God in the form of a golden calf or a bull. This was intended to symbolize the God who brought them out of Egypt. They were trying to honor God with what they thought was a fitting symbol of His great strength. But that symbol actually insulted God, because it fell short of depicting His true glory. That symbol couldn't even begin to capture God's moral character, goodness, justice, and patience.

God is limitless in His power and His knowledge. We can't confine God spatially; He's everywhere at once. We can't confine Him in time, either; He always has been and He always will be without beginning or end. How could we ever put all of that into a statue or a painting or even a movie?

If these images distort the glory of God, they also mislead people. They pervert our thoughts of Him. Michelangelo was a great artist, but did God the Father have a long flowing gray beard and a pinkish tunic? Every image or likeness of God we create falls short, distorting the glory of God and misleading people as to what He is really like.

## THE SCALES ARE TIPPED TOWARD MERCY

Man-made images of God arouse God's jealousy. Exodus 20:5 says, "You shall not bow down to them or worship them; for I, the LORD your God, am a jealous God." God's jealousy is a hard concept to understand, because we think of jealousy in such negative terms. That's why we call it "the green-eyed monster." But we all know that while some jealousy is indeed rooted in selfishness, there is an appropriate kind of jealousy that's rooted in passionate love. God's jealousy is not the insecure, insane, or possessive human jealousy we all disdain; instead, it's the intensely caring devotion He has to the objects of his love. A God who isn't jealous over His people is as contemptible as a husband who doesn't care when his wife is unfaithful to him. But why would God be jealous of our depictions of Him?

Keep in mind that God is jealous for His name. Part of God's jealousy is His zeal to protect and maintain His own glory. When we use an image of God in our worship, we rouse His jealous passion, because we're worshiping a distorted image of who He is. God cares as much about our worship of Him being pure as He does about it being exclusive.

Man-made representations of God have consequences for ourselves and for those around us. The second commandment goes on to spell this out: "I, the LORD your God, am a jealous God, punishing the children for the sin of the parents to the third and fourth generation of those who hate me, but showing love to a thousand generations of those who love me and keep my commandments" (Exodus 20:5–6).

Those who make images of the true God and use them in worship will end up not only with a distorted image of God but also with a distorted image of what He wants from them. And that will get passed on to their children and grandchildren and great-grandchildren. God isn't saying He's going to punish your family and your descendants for your sin; He's saying that your choice to worship an image of Him will infect your family with a disease that results in their having a distorted image of God, even hating Him. It's a serious and dangerous thing to pass on to your children a wrong conception of God.

But there is another contrast here. The lovingkindness of God extends out to a thousand generations toward those who love Him and keep His commands! God is far more interested in blessing people than in judging people. God's character is weighted toward mercy. "His anger lasts only a moment, but his favor lasts a lifetime" (Psalm 30:5). What a great motive for keeping the second commandment! We infect a thousand generations with a love and obedience toward God.

## HOW TO BREAK THE SECOND COMMANDMENT

You might be wondering how all of this might apply to us today. If you were to take a tour of many church sanctuaries, you wouldn't find a lot of physical representations of God. But you might not be looking close enough. In the last chapter I mentioned "idols of the heart," anything that can capture our heart's first affection, like family, money, or sports. In a similar way, it's easy to break the second commandment with a heart disposition that tries to worship the *right God* in the *wrong way*. I believe we can do that in several ways.

First, we worship the right God in the wrong way whenever

we place *seeing* above *hearing.* Moses reminded Israel that upon Mount Sinai they couldn't see God, but they could hear Him. "Then the Lord spoke to you out of the fire. You heard the sound of words but saw no form; there was only a voice" (Deuteronomy 4:12). The way God revealed himself at Mount Sinai wasn't through a visible image but through an audible word. This tells us something about how God wants to be worshiped. Instead of looking, He wants us listening. This is sometimes hard for us to swallow, because we live in such a visual age. To accommodate that, we bring big screens into the church and have banners and props and drama. Many of us are more visual learners, and we feel that these kinds of things communicate to us more powerfully than the spoken word. Visual communication isn't necessarily bad unless it somehow distracts us from hearing the Word of God.

Second, we worship the right God in the wrong way whenever we make a particular *expression* of worship more important than the *essence* of worship. The expression of worship has to do with style; the essence of worship has to do with God. We all have preferences in worship style, but whenever our focus shifts from the person of God to the style of worship we're in danger of breaking the second commandment. God is bigger than any worship style. Whether it's our preference or not, as long as worship exalts the true God and focuses our attention and adoration on Him, we should thank God for it.

Third, we worship the right God in the wrong way whenever we imagine God to be someone we can manipulate. One of the reasons people in history loved to make images of God was that it allowed them to manipulate Him. The thinking was that if they did this or that, then they would be able to get the god to do what they wanted. We tend to do the same thing. We want a user-friendly God who will adapt to our desires and purposes. We think, *If I do this, He'll do that. If I pray a certain way, He'll give me what I ask for. If I have enough faith, He'll heal me or make me rich. If I follow God's priorities for parenting, my children will grow up and be good Christians.* Whenever we try to manipulate God with actions, we're breaking the second commandment because we're imagining Him to be something he's not. God won't be captured, contained, assigned, or managed by anyone or anything.

Fourth, we worship the right God in the wrong way whenever we worship God for some of His attributes but leave out others. Some people want a God of love. So they focus on His love, compassion, and mercy but leave out things like His holiness, His justice, and the reality of both heaven and hell. Others want a big God who is holy and sovereign and far above and beyond any of us. They leave out the idea that God is also close to us; He's not just our ruler—He's also our Abba Father (See Romans 8:15).

Fifth, we worship the right God in the wrong way whenever

we divorce our concept of God from the product He produces in our lives. Worshiping God in the right way affects the way we live. Worship brings us into an encounter with the living God, and that encounter will change us if it's authentic. We live in a society in which many people claim to have a relationship with Jesus Christ, but when they are asked about how that relationship really affects their lives and their decisions, they fall silent. If you or I think we can attend worship services, sing a few songs, pray a few prayers, feel some warm feelings, listen to good sermons, but then leave and live the way we want to live instead of the way He has told us to live, we're worshiping the right God in the wrong way.

## THE DEEP MYSTERY

There's a deep mystery behind the second commandment: the God who told us not to make an image of himself has, in fact, given us an image of himself. Jesus is called "the image of the invisible God" (Colossians 1:15). The writer of Hebrews called Jesus "the exact representation of [God's] being" (Hebrews 1:3). And Jesus himself said, "Anyone who has seen me has seen the Father" (John 14:9).

We don't worship a physical image of Jesus, but in order to worship the right God in the right way, we need to focus on the person of Jesus. When we focus on the person of Jesus, we find ourselves becoming more and more like Him. This brings us back right where we started. Privilege and responsibility go hand in hand: When you worship the right God in the right way, your worship will be centered on the person and work of Jesus. And that always leads to a transformed life.

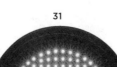

# 3

# CALLING ON GOD'S POWERFUL NAME[2]

Imagine if everybody on the planet obeyed the Ten Commandments. The world would be a much better place. There would be no stealing or murder. There would be no adultery; marriages would remain faithful. Children would honor their father and mother. Everyone in our society—from ordinary people to sports heroes to business leaders and politicians—would tell the truth. Nobody would bear false witness against anyone else. And without the need to covet your neighbor's spouse or his house or his new car, we would all live with deep contentment.

But what about the third commandment? "You shall not misuse the name of the Lord your God, for the Lord will not hold anyone guiltless who misuses his name" (Deuteronomy 5:11). Would keeping this commandment make any significant difference in our world?

Many people think, *This just means that I should never say, "Oh my God."* But this commandment isn't concerned with small matters. This is a weighty commandment. It's also a wonderful, liberating commandment. Obeying the third commandment on a consistent basis would make our society flourish with goodness, and it would also radically change your life for the better.

Bible scholar Alan Cole said, "The whole of the Ten Commandments are really the explanation of God's name." In other words, all of the commandments offer an explanation of the third commandment about the power and beauty of God's name.

## THE POWER OF A NAME

In Shakespeare's play *Romeo and Juliet*, Juliet says, "What's in a name? That which we call a rose by any other name would smell as sweet." Said another way, it doesn't matter what you call something or someone, because the name doesn't matter. What matters is the thing itself—the flower or the person represented by the name—but not the name itself.

In the Hebrew culture, however, a name was everything. A name represented the very essence and presence of a person. A person's identity was bound up in his or her name. A name contained power.

Names still hold power today. Joe Paterno, the successful and then disgraced coach for the Penn State football team, sobbed while meeting with his coaches the day after the university fired him. According to an article about Paterno in the September 2012 issue of *Gentlemen's Quarterly* magazine, the Hall of Fame coach was quoted as saying, "My name, I have spent my whole life trying to make that name mean something. Now it's gone."[3]

Without a name, who are you? You get your identity from a name. Why did your parents choose your name? Who would you be without your name? Who would you be if no one knew what to call you, if you didn't know what to call yourself? There's a world of difference when you say, "Hey, Joan" instead of "Hey, waitress" or "Hey, Bill" instead of "Hey, Officer."

In the ancient world, when you called on the name of a god, you wanted a specific response from that god, a response that reflected the identity of that god. Baal was the god of the rain. You called on his name if you wanted rain. Asherah was the goddess of fertility. You called on her name if you wanted to have a baby. When the ancient Israelites used God's name, the name of "the LORD your God," they were calling upon all of who God is. When the Hebrew people used God's name, they understood that.

## THE MISUSE OF GOD'S NAME

Now that we understand something about the power of a name, what does it mean to misuse God's name, or as the New King James Version puts it, to "take the name of the LORD your God in vain" (Exodus 20:7)? The Israelites misused God's name whenever they carelessly used it in taking an oath or making a promise they didn't keep, whenever they mixed their worship of

God with worship of the false gods that surrounded them, or whenever they used God's name for their own gain to get ahead.

We have our own ways of violating the third commandment. As a matter of fact, the Hebrews would never have dreamed of how God's name is misused in our society. They carefully guarded how and when they spoke the name of the Lord. Stephen L. Carter, author of *God's Name in Vain*, writes:

> In truth, there is probably no country in the Western world where people use God's name quite as much, or quite as publicly, or for quite as many purposes, as we Americans do—the Third Commandment notwithstanding. Few candidates for office are able to end their speeches without asking God to bless their audience, or the nation, or the great work we are undertaking, but everybody is sure the other side is insincere. . . . Athletes thank God, often on television, after scoring the winning touchdown, because, like politicians, they like to think God is on their side. Churches erect huge billboards and take out ads in the paper. . . . Everybody who wants to change America, and everybody who wants not to, understands the nation's love affair with God's name, which is why everybody invokes it.[4]

One of the main ways Americans use, or rather misuse, God's name is by using it as a swear word. Many people in our culture respond to maddening or even joyful circumstances with an outburst of "Oh my God!" or "Jesus Christ!" Most people wouldn't treat their mother's name that way, but for some reason many assume it's acceptable to treat God's name with such blatant disrespect. As a Christian, that's the name that saved your soul. According to Jesus, this careless way of using God's name has consequences. In Matthew 12:36 Jesus said, "But I tell you that everyone will have to give account on the day of judgment for every empty word they have spoken."

Sometimes we diminish God's name by building up our own name. We are called to live for God's name rather than our own name. You and I fulfill our God-given design when our lives build up His name and His fame. This commandment challenges us to ask a searching question about our own spiritual lives: *Whose name am I building up?* The only way you discover what's unique about yourself, the only way you discover your true identity and name is by building up God's name. That's what you're designed to do. Imagine how much better our world would be if all of us were to quit worrying about our own name and instead focus our energies on building up God's name.

Finally, we also violate the third commandment when we treat it merely as a negative statement and neglect its positive character. All of the Ten Commandments can be stated in the positive. These commandments affirm life; they're a roadmap to a new, free, wonderful way to live. There are hundreds of positive ways we can use God's name. His name can be spoken, worshiped, trusted, celebrated, adored, shouted, whispered, honored, cherished, exalted, and enjoyed. God has many names we can use: God Almighty, Shepherd, King, Rock, Healer, Provider, Holy One, Creator, Redeemer, and Most High God. In the name of God we can pray, heal, protect, preach, baptize, and move mountains. Psalm 8:1 says, "LORD, our Lord, how majestic is your name in all the earth!"

## THESE AREN'T "TEN SUGGESTIONS"

During a commencement address at Duke University, veteran journalist Ted Koppel reminded the bright, young college grads that "what Moses brought down from Mount Sinai were not the Ten Suggestions."[5] As His people, God expects us to obey His commandments, and in particular to obey the third commandment by making good use of His name. But we don't always keep the third commandment. We sometimes fail to use God's name the way He commands us to use it.

But breaking this commandment comes with a consequence, a penalty. The rest of Exodus 20:7 continues: "The LORD will not hold anyone guiltless who misuses his name." What we do with God's name will determine what He does with us.

There is someone who has kept the third commandment perfectly—someone who never took God's name in vain, someone who lived and died perfectly honoring God's name. His name is

Jesus. And Jesus changes everything. Jesus transforms the third commandment, turning it into something that gives life for humanity. Throughout His ministry, Jesus always called God "Father." That name reflects the kind of intimacy Jesus shared with God the Father. And through the cross, He opened the way for us to share that same kind of intimacy. Through Christ, we can know God on a "first-name basis." We can call Him Father. Moses said to the Israelites: "You shall not misuse the name of the LORD your God" (Exodus 20:7). But Jesus says to all of us, "When you pray, say: 'Father, hallowed be your name' " (Luke 11:2).

This sets Christianity apart from all other religions. The God of the Bible doesn't wait for us to reach out to Him; He reaches out to us first. This is the God who out of His great love for us sacrificed His only Son in order to make us His sons and daughters. The Father and the Son planned it so that through His work on the cross Jesus would fulfill the prophetic words from Isaiah 43:6–7: "Bring my sons from afar and my daughters from the ends of the earth—everyone who is called by my name, whom I created for my glory, whom I formed and made." When we trust Jesus, God becomes our Father.

So the third commandment also reminds us that we are sons and daughters of the Father. Jesus has taken away the awful penalty of the third commandment, He's taken away our guilt, and He calls us into an abundant life of honoring and enjoying our Father's name.

## EXPOSE YOUR FEARS

So how do we do it? We still have a commandment before us: don't misuse the name of the Lord your God (the name of your Father). Stated positively it means that we should honor this name. But how do we do bring honor to His name? There are many ways to obey this commandment, but perhaps there's one way that pleases God the most: we obey the third commandment when we trust His name and when we surrender to Him in a life of love and trust.

While I was in college, I worked one summer at a Young Life camp in the Colorado Rockies. My job was to drive a jeep full of high school kids from the camp at 8,000 feet to a little chalet at 13,000 feet. The road was incredibly narrow; it was cut into mountain in such a way that if I lost control I could end up rolling down the mountain, endangering the lives of those kids. I quickly found myself in a dilemma. On the one hand, I was frightened almost to the point of paralysis. On the other hand, I knew God had called me to serve there that summer. I knew I could trust Him as my Father. I knew I could stand on Him as my Rock. In short, I knew I could trust in His Name. Eighteenth-century Bible scholar Matthew Henry explained how this works when he said, "Those who make God and His name their praise, may make God and His name their trust."

After a couple of faith-stretching weeks, I did something

that for me was really hard. I exposed my fears to the people I was working with. I told them I was petrified to drive up and down that mountain. I asked them to pray for me. And they did. Within days I was able to loosen my grip on the wheel. I was able to enjoy the people in the jeep. I experienced the joy and strength of trusting in God's name as I drove. I learned through that experience that I could trust in the name of God.

When you trust in God your Father, who cares for you and gives you strength to face any challenge, you are keeping the spirit of the third commandment.

# 4

# REDISCOVERING A REST-FILLED LIFE

While I was leading some pastor training in the Philippines, I divided the pastors into small groups and asked them to talk about various things in their lives. One of the questions focused on what they enjoyed doing in their spare time—what they did to relax. As I walked from group to group listening to their responses, I kept hearing the same thing: "Spare time? I don't have any spare time."

A lot of us feel that way—even little kids. A photographer was snapping pictures of first-graders at an elementary school, making small talk to put the kids at ease. "What are you going to be when you grow up?" he asked one little girl. "Tired," she said.

It's true; a lot of adults are tired. I like what Will Rogers said, "Half our life is spent trying to find something to do with the time we have rushed through life trying to save." We are fooling ourselves if we think this nonstop pace makes us more effective. The average office worker gets 220 messages a day—

e-mails, memos, phone calls, interruptions, and ads. No wonder a survey of more than 1,300 managers on four continents found that "one-third of managers suffer from ill health as a direct consequence of stress associated with information overload. This figure increases to 43 percent with senior managers."

## THE FATIGUE THAT KILLS

Sometimes our exhaustion makes us dangerous. Some of the most notorious industrial accidents of the modern world—*Exxon Valdez*, Three Mile Island, Chernobyl—occurred in the middle of the night. In the *Challenger* space shuttle disaster, NASA officials made the decision to go ahead with the launch after working twenty hours straight and getting only two to three hours of sleep the night before. Their error in judgment cost the lives of seven astronauts. We ignore our need for rest and renewal at the peril of others and ourselves.

And perhaps the greatest danger is the harm we do to our own souls. Could this be another form of idolatry? Barbara Brown Taylor writes:

Some of us have made an idol of exhaustion. The only time we know we have done enough is when we're running on empty and when the ones we love most are the ones we see the least. When we lie down to sleep at night, we offer our full appointment calendars to God in lieu of prayer, believing that God—who is as busy as we are—will surely understand.[6]

So what's the answer to this problem? How do we find rest and renewal, not just for our bodies but also for our souls? The answer is in the fourth commandment. In Deuteronomy God said:

*Observe the Sabbath day by keeping it holy, as the LORD your God has commanded you. Six days you shall labor and do all your work, but the seventh day is a sabbath to the LORD your God. On it you shall not do any work, neither you, nor your son or your daughter, nor your male or female servant, nor your ox, your donkey or any of your animals, nor any foreigner residing in your towns. (5:12–14)*

How do we find rest and renewal for our souls? Observe the principle of the Sabbath. This chapter is organized around three simple questions about the Sabbath: 1. What does it mean? 2. Why was it given? 3. How do we keep it?

## EVERYBODY STOP!

We're told to observe or to guard or to remember the Sabbath day, the seventh day of the week. Exodus says, "The LORD blessed the Sabbath day and made it holy" (20:11). God made it holy, but we have to keep it holy. When something is holy, it is different, unique, or special. God made the Sabbath that way, but we have to keep it that way. The Sabbath is to be treated with special care and significance.

So how do we do this? The first step is pretty clear: *stop working*. The word *sabbath* means "to cease" or "to stop." This commandment was for everyone—children, slaves, even animals. Even before the Ten Commandments were given, as the Israelites were on their way to Mount Sinai, God provided manna six days out of seven. Every day they went out to gather the manna, but the seventh day was a day of rest. We also keep this day holy by stopping our work and resting.

But to keep something holy in the biblical sense also means to dedicate it for worship. The Sabbath wasn't just a day to rest; it was also a day to worship and a day to replenish the soul. This is the positive side of the fourth commandment. Leviticus calls the Sabbath "a day of sacred assembly" (23:3), meaning it was a time for God's people to gather for worship. It wasn't just a day to rest; it was a day to pray. The Puritans called the Sabbath the "market day of the soul." On the other days of the week you do ordinary business, but on this day you do spiritual business, trading in the currency of heaven. It's a day to rejuvenate not only the body but also the spirit. Eugene Peterson explained the Sabbath this way:

Sabbath: uncluttered time and space to distance ourselves

from the frenzy of our own activities so we can see what God was and is doing. If we don't regularly quit work one day a week, we take ourselves far too seriously. The moral sweat pouring off our brow blinds us to the primal action of God in and around us.[7]

## MORE THAN MACHINES

In part, God gave us the fourth commandment because He himself took a Sabbath. In Exodus 20:11, after God gave the command, Moses explained its rationale: "For in six days the LORD made the heavens and the earth, the sea, and all that is in them, but he rested on the seventh day. Therefore the LORD blessed the Sabbath day and made it holy." We're meant to keep the Sabbath because God, after creating the heavens and the earth, stopped working on the seventh day and rested.

Moses' words imply that if God stopped working on the seventh day, we too should rest. Of course, God didn't need to rest. He chose to do so as an example for us. Notice that this took place before the fall of man, before sin entered into the world. The Sabbath was a part of the paradise Adam and Eve enjoyed. They were to subdue the earth, but God also gave them the Sabbath. Not only that, but the idea of Sabbath existed before God gave Israel the law. The Sabbath principle isn't something that applies solely to the Israelites; the Sabbath came before the

Israelites. God built this rhythm of work-rest, work-rest into the fabric of time and creation. We all have a need to observe this rhythm, because without it our lives go sour.

We experience this most noticeably in our daily rhythm of work and sleep. Try to go without sleep for too long and watch out, you'll pay for it. George MacDonald said, "Sleep is God's contrivance for giving us the help he couldn't get into us when we were awake." We all have to sleep. But, unfortunately, keeping to a weekly rhythm of work and rest isn't quite as easy, so it has to be commanded.

Deuteronomy 5:15 adds another reason for keeping the Sabbath: For 400 years Israel labored as slaves in Egypt without a Sabbath. Then God came along and gave them rest by delivering them from that slavery. Lest Israel did to their slaves and animals and foreigners what the Egyptians did to them, they were to keep the Sabbath. Israel was to show the same mercy that God had shown to them.

This shows a profoundly humanitarian aspect to Sabbath-keeping. People are more than just machines, good only for what they can produce. The Sabbath protects people from being reduced to units of production. During the aftermath of the French Revolution, the Sabbath was abolished, being substituted with one day's rest in ten. But apparently the experiment was a disaster; men and women crumbled under the strain and animals literally collapsed in the streets. People need Sabbath because they're people, not machines.

## THE SABBATH FULFILLER

Some think that the fourth commandment is the one commandment that's no longer relevant, because the New Testament doesn't say anywhere that we have an obligation to keep the Sabbath. So if we're going to answer the question of how we keep this commandment today, we have to start with what Jesus taught about the Sabbath.

In the New Testament, Jesus practiced keeping the Sabbath—but with a whole new understanding of it. In Luke 4:16 we read, "He went to Nazareth, where he had been brought up, and on the Sabbath day he went into the synagogue, as was his custom. He stood up to read." Jesus was in the habit of observing at least one aspect of the Sabbath—the need for public worship. You might say that Jesus observed the Sabbath by going to church.

But if you look at the Gospels, you can also see that Jesus had a different understanding of the Sabbath than the religious leaders of the day. One day Jesus was passing through the grain fields on the Sabbath. His disciples were hungry, so they began to pick the heads of grain. The Pharisees saw this and were upset. They had created a very elaborate code of restrictions of what you could and couldn't do on the Sabbath. They asked Jesus why

His disciples were breaking the Sabbath law. Jesus responded by reminding them what King David did when he and his friends became hungry: they entered the temple and ate the consecrated bread, which wasn't lawful for anyone to eat except the priests. And then Jesus said, "The Sabbath was made for man, not man for the Sabbath" (Mark 2:27).

The Pharisees had added so many restrictions to the Sabbath that it ended up being a burden. Its purpose was to give rest and spiritual refreshment, but in their legalism they had made it into a form of slavery. In their desire to protect the Sabbath, they corrupted it. Jesus didn't throw out the Sabbath; instead, he restored its true meaning.

As we consider the practice of the early church in the book of Acts and the Epistles, we see that something had happened to change their view of the Sabbath. The Jewish Sabbath, which they were accustomed to keeping, was on the seventh day of the week. But Jesus was raised from the dead not on the seventh day but on the first day of the week—Sunday. It seems the early church felt the freedom to switch days and make Sunday instead of Saturday the special day. So we read in Acts 20:7, "On the first day of the week we came together to break bread. Paul spoke to the people and, because he intended to leave the next day, kept on talking until midnight."

Notice that the church gathered together on the first day of the week, not the seventh. That's why in 1 Corinthians 16:2 Paul says, "On the first day of every week, each one of you should set aside a sum of money in keeping with your income, saving it up, so that when I come no collections will have to be made." Paul says take offering on the first day of every week because that's when the church gathered for worship.

Finally, in Revelation 1:10 John says, "On the Lord's Day I was in the Spirit, and I heard behind me a loud voice like a trumpet." John doesn't tell us when the Lord's Day was, but we have good reason to believe it was the first day of the week. Isn't it interesting that John calls it the "Lord's Day"? Even for New Testament believers there was one day among seven set aside as uniquely the Lord's.

But we have to be careful. This doesn't mean that the New Testament church rigidly observed every rule that the Old Testament law laid down about the Sabbath—only on Sunday instead of Saturday. In fact, Paul reprimands the Colossians for keeping a legalistic Sabbath. He says, "Do not let anyone judge you by what you eat or drink, or with regard to a religious festival, a New Moon celebration or a Sabbath day. These are a shadow of the things that were to come; the reality, however, is found in Christ" (Colossians 2:16–17). When he says, "The reality, however, is found in Christ," what does he mean? Somehow the Sabbath looked forward to Christ; Jesus fulfills the Sabbath. The Sabbath is all about ceasing from our work and about resting. This has both a physical and spiritual application. Christ had fulfilled the law. His death and resurrection freed us from having to work to earn His favor and love. We can rest completely in Him for our righteousness. Hebrews says, "For anyone who enters God's rest also rests from their works, just as God did from his" (4:10). If we trust Christ, we have rested from our works. In a spiritual sense, we can enjoy Sabbath rest seven days a week.

Christ has set us free from the rigid, legalistic Sabbath-keeping, but we don't ignore the original purpose of the Sabbath. The Christian Sabbath, while not being restricted to Sunday or the Lord's Day, is still a day for rest, a day for worship, and a day for showing mercy.

## A DAY OF REST

The Sabbath principle gives us a day of rest. It's a day to catch our breath—a day not to go to work. If you're a full-time homemaker, it's a day for you to have a break from the grind of cooking and cleaning and getting things done. If you're a full-time student, it's a day for you to rest from the burden of endless books to read, projects to finish, and papers to write. Whatever work you do, stop it once a week and relax. Instead of working, do things that refuel your body, your mind, your relationships, and your soul. If you like movies, go see a good film. If you like to ride your bike, do that. If you like to hike, take a long one.

If you like to read, go for it. If you like to garden, plant some flowers.

J. I. Packer said that we should "choose the leisure activities that bring us closest to God, to people, to beauty, and to all that ennobles." The important thing is to detach yourself from your everyday work. The Sabbath is a time to say, "I'm not a human doing but a human being. I'm more than my work." It takes faith to do this. You have to say, "I'll stop working and trust God that the work I could be doing on this day will somehow get done. God will see to that."

## A DAY OF WORSHIP

Second, the Sabbath is a day uniquely blessed for the refreshment of God's people as they gather together and worship the Lord and hear His Word. The Sabbath is not just a "day off." The sole goal of a day off is leisure, fun, and play. Isn't it interesting that we live in a culture obsessed with leisure and recreation, but very few people are rested? We actually have a leisure industry—and very profitable one at that! Yet we have more exhaustion, fatigue, and burnout than ever before. We've lost a biblical view of rest—rest that includes a recognition and appreciation of God, and the rejuvenation that only comes through worship of the living God and fellowship with His people. As Albert Schweitzer said, "If your soul has no Sunday, it becomes an orphan."

## A DAY TO SHOW MERCY

Finally, the Sabbath is a day to show mercy. That's what Jesus did. It's a great day to welcome a hurting person into your home, visit someone in the hospital, feed someone who is hungry, or just spend time with someone who is lonely.

Sometimes this mercy begins with how we run our businesses. When people are required to work seven days straight for sixty to seventy hours per week, they start to feel used, regardless of how much money they make. If you're an employer, recognize this reality. Your employees are more than machines that exist for your benefit.

Truett Cathy (1921–2014), the founder of Chick-fil-A restaurants, was a successful businessman. The longtime CEO of the nearly 2,000 Chick-fil-A restaurants declared in 1948 that his restaurants would remain closed on Sunday. He didn't mind losing millions of dollars of business to honor the Lord's Day. He recognized that his employees needed rest. He showed mercy to them by freeing them from work one day a week.

## THE BETTER WAY

Someone told the story of a man who was approached by a beggar on the street. The man reached into his pocket to see what he had. He found seven dollars. Feeling sorry for the beggar, he held out six bills and said, "You can have this." Not only did the beggar grab the six dollars, but with the other hand, he hit the guy in the face and grabbed the seventh dollar as well.

What do you think about that beggar's actions? How could he possibly be so ungrateful and greedy? But is that beggar all that different from the person (possibly us!) who has been rescued by the grace of Jesus but then grabs not just six days a week but all seven. There's a better way to live, a deeper, more peaceful life centered on the fourth commandment. God gave us the Sabbath, and now we have to guard it, keeping it as a day of rest, a day for worship, and a day for showing mercy. How freeing it is to know that God has provided this day of rest and rejuvenation for us in our weekly calendar!

## 5

# MAKING PARENTS "WEIGHTY"

"Honor your father and your mother" (Exodus 20:12). Most of us know the fifth commandment by heart. But how does this commandment speak to us today? So many broken homes, so many abusive homes. Unlike in Moses' times, we have fragments of our extended families spread across the country. Our entire culture caters to youth while marginalizing senior citizens. It's easy to assume that this command comes from a bygone era that's totally out of touch with the reality of our lives today.

One man offered the following complaint:

Youth today have luxury. They have bad manners, contempt for authority, no respect for older people, and talk nonsense when they should work. Young people do not stand up any longer when adults enter the room. They contradict their parents, talk too much in company . . . and tyrannize their elders.

Surprisingly, that was written by Socrates 400 years before Christ! It reminds us that every generation of young people has had issues with their parents.

## THE FIRST AND PRIMARY RELATIONSHIP

This commandment is given a prominent place in the list of ten. Traditionally, the first four commandments are distinguished from the last six. The first table of the law deals with our relationship with God. The second table has six commands that deal with our relationship with people. The first four teach us how to love God; the last six teach us how to love our neighbor. Love for God has to come first. We can't truly love one another unless we love God. But isn't it significant that in telling us how to treat our neighbor, God starts with our own family?

Loving our neighbor starts at home, and home life starts with how we relate to our parents. This relationship is foundational to all other relationships. Augustine recognized this when he said, "If anyone fails to honor his parents, is there anyone he will spare?" Augustine was implying that the relationship between parent and child is the first and primary relationship. It's not only the foundation for all our other relationships; it's also the foundation for human society. Our family is our first hospital, first school, first government, and first church. If we don't honor authority at home, we'll have a hard time respecting it anywhere, and society will crumble.

## "WEIGHTY" PARENTS

Because of its importance, we need to study this commandment carefully. The first and most important word is *honor*. The Hebrew word literally means "heavy" or "weighty." It's the word the Old Testament uses to describe the glory of God, the weightiness of His person. Like a nugget of gold, the heavier something is, the more valuable it is. When someone is weighty, we take that person seriously. To honor our parents is to give due weight to their position, to hold them in high esteem, to value them. When we give weight to something, we give it our time, energy, and attention. How much weight do you give to your work? Your finances? Your favorite sports team? Your health or your friends? These are things to which we typically give time, energy, and attention and on which we place the most value.

Notice that this commandment includes both fathers and mothers. In other places in the Bible there is an emphasis on the father as the leader of a household. But this never means that mothers deserve less honor than fathers. In certain ways, a mother can be easier for a child to take advantage of, but God says mothers deserve equal respect. And one of the ways a father leads his family is by honoring his wife and insisting that his children honor her (their mother) as well.

## AN ADDED BONUS CLAUSE

Parents deserve to be honored because of the sacrifices they make. They deserve to be honored because of the life experience they have. The Bible even goes so far as to say that when a child honors his parents, it's the right thing to do, and it pleases the Lord (see Ephesians 6:1).

It's not just that parents deserve to be honored; it's also that by learning to honor them we learn to honor authority in general. The sixteenth-century Heidelberg Catechism says the fifth commandment requires "that I show honor, love, and faithfulness to my mother and father and to all who are set in authority over me." So when God tells us to respect our parents, by implication He's also telling us to respect government authority, church authority, and even those in authority over us at work.

These are all good reasons to keep the fifth commandment, but the best reason is found right in the commandment itself: "Honor your father and your mother, so that you may live long in the land the LORD your God is giving you" (Exodus 20:12). In other words, obeying the fifth commandment serves our best interest. That's why in Ephesians 6:2, Paul says this is "the first commandment with a promise." Maybe God knows how hard it is at times to honor our parents, so He attaches a reward to it.

Proverbs says, "My son, do not forget my teaching, but keep my commands in your heart, for they will prolong your life many years and bring you peace and prosperity" (Proverbs 3:1–2). That's a commentary on the fifth commandment. Do you want life and peace? Then listen as your parents teach you about a

God who loves you and sent His Son to die for you. For many people, faith in Christ has been a direct result of listening to their parents' instruction.

## HOW TO HONOR FLAWED PARENTS

But this isn't everyone's story—and it certainly wasn't my story. Many people have also had dysfunctional or even abusive parents. What does this commandment mean for them? The Bible mentions several dysfunctional parents. It started with Adam and Eve, who had a son who murdered his brother. Abraham told a government official that his wife Sarah was his sister—just to save his own skin. Rebekah manipulated and deceived her husband Isaac in order to secure her favorite son's future. Dishonorable parents are nothing new.

Maybe the best example in Scripture of how to handle dysfunctional parents comes from the story of two best friends—David and Jonathan. Consider their story: David and Jonathan were spiritual brothers, bound together early in life on the battlefield against the Philistines. But they had bigger problems than the Philistines. Jonathan's father, King Saul, was an angry, insecure, unpredictable man. During one battle, Saul swore to curse any soldier who ate anything before he avenged his enemies. Jonathan didn't hear his father's oath, and he ate some honey. When Saul heard of it, he said to his son, "You shall surely die" (1 Samuel 14:44 NKJV). The other soldiers intervened to save

Jonathan's life, but that shows the kind of man Saul was—he threatened to kill his own son over a mouthful of food.

Saul treated David even worse. At first he loved him, but then he became jealous of him. David was becoming more famous than Saul, so one day Saul tried to nail David to the wall with a spear. When he failed, he then tried to get him killed in battle. He even ordered his son Jonathan to kill him, which clearly put Jonathan in a bind. He knew he was supposed to honor his father, but he also knew murder was wrong. So he did the right thing: he honored God by disobeying his father. He warned David of what his father was up to, and then he confronted his father and said, "Why then would you do wrong to an innocent man like David by killing him for no reason?" (1 Samuel 19:5). In doing this, Jonathan wasn't dishonoring his father—he was honoring him by trying to get him to do the right thing. As adults, the command to honor parents doesn't mean we do everything they tell us to do. We have to honor God first. Sometimes we honor our parents the most by trying to preserve their honor and keep them from doing something that will dishonor God.

The command to honor parents doesn't mean that we never set up boundaries in our relationships with them. Submitting to authority never means subjecting ourselves to violence or abuse. There are times to say to a parent, "Because of how you've broken my trust over and over again, at least for now I can't be in a close relationship with you." You honor them more by doing that than by allowing them to continue in their destructive ways.

## YOU NEVER OUTGROW THIS COMMANDMENT

The fifth commandment is for *children*. God wants children to obey their parents, to listen respectfully, to obey their words, because God knows what's best for them.

The fifth commandment is for *teenagers*. Middle school or high school culture gives teenagers the following message: "Your parents don't get you. They're old and out of touch. Therefore, they'll just make you unhappy." But God offers a different perspective. God says, "I gave you your parents. Believe it or not, they're what you need—even with all their faults and flaws. And no one knows you better than they do. So honor them by accepting them and thanking God for them. Honor them by speaking well of them to your friends. Honor them by listening to their perspective. Honor them by telling them the truth."

The fifth commandment is for *young adults*. A strange thing happens at around age twenty. All of a sudden, parents become okay again. But young adults also start to see parents for who they really are, including their broken places. Ultimately, young adults have to start making their own decisions about major life issues, but they can still honor their parents by seeking their counsel and blessing in those decisions.

When I first decided to become a pastor, my parents didn't

support me. As a matter of fact, they thought I was a little crazy. At that point I was a disappointment to them. But I felt God had called me, so that was a decision where I had to honor God first. Jesus said, "Anyone who loves their father or mother more than me is not worthy of me" (Matthew 10:37). Our commitment to obey God always comes first. At the same time, before I married my wife, I sought their counsel and blessing, which they gave me. Even though they weren't believers at the time, I found that my parents usually gave me very wise counsel.

Finally, the fifth commandment is for *adults*. It's for people in their thirties, forties, fifties, and even sixties. Quite a few scholars believe this command was primarily meant for adults with older parents. Remember, in those days there was no social security system, and several generations would live together under one roof. If your children didn't take care of you, you were sunk.

Honoring your parents means taking responsibility for their care. Surveys show that barely half of Americans think it's their job to care for their elderly parents. When Jesus saw Pharisees refusing to care for their parents because of money they said was devoted to God, he accused them of breaking the fifth commandment. Honoring your parents means that you make sure they're taken care of. It also means you continue to value them by spending time with them, talking and listening to them. Too many people in my generation are just waiting around for an inheritance. This command reminds us that as adults, our primary role is not to take from our parents but to give to them. When we honor our parents in this way, we honor God (see Leviticus 19:32).

## JESUS: PERFECT CHILD, PERFECT SAVIOR

The sad fact is, no matter what age we are, none of us have kept the fifth commandment perfectly. Have you ever lied to your parents? Did you ever speak poorly of them? Have you weighed their advice lightly instead of heavily? Have you ever felt as if they were in your way and demanded too much from you? Not one of us has been a perfect child.

Except for Jesus. Jesus honored His parents. As a child, we're told, "He went down to Nazareth with [his parents] and was obedient to them" (Luke 2:51). That doesn't mean there wasn't any strain. As an adolescent, there was tension when He stayed behind at the temple instead of going home with His parents (see Luke 2:41–50). Later, there was a situation when He kept preaching instead of stopping to visit His family (see Luke 8:19–21). But Jesus honored His parents right to the end of His life. He couldn't personally care for His mother in her old age, but He saw to it that she was provided for by asking His friend John to be a son to her (see John 19:26–27). From the manger to the cross, Jesus honored His parents.

As we strive to keep the fifth commandment, let's remember

that Jesus is the only One who ever kept it perfectly. Because of Him, we can give grace to our kids and give grace to our parents. Jesus is the perfect Savior because He was the perfect child.

# 6

# CHERISHING THE DIGNITY OF LIFE[8]

The sixth commandment is another short, straightforward instruction: "You shall not murder" (Exodus 20:13). At this point in examining the Ten Commandments, many people heave a sigh of relief. *Finally,* they think, *a commandment that I know I haven't broken yet! I can honestly say that I haven't murdered anyone.* But as we explore the deeper dimensions of this commandment, it forces us to ask questions like these: *Have I ever harbored bitterness and anger toward someone else? Have I ever secretly wished that a certain person would get seriously injured or maybe even killed? Have I ever been so mad that I've said, "I'd like to kill him"?* This commandment proves it: We're all murderers.

## MURDER IS ALWAYS WRONG

In the original Hebrew language, this verse is only two words: "No murder." That's it. While everyone agrees what *no* means, we're often confused about the second word—*murder.* Does this include all forms of killing? What about the killing of animals? What about war and capital punishment? Are those forms of murder?

This passage uses a very specific Hebrew word, *ratsach*, which refers to *premeditative killing*. It is used forty-seven times in the Old Testament, and it always refers to the intentional and violent killing of a person. That is why the word *murder* and not *kill* is the correct translation of this verse. One can accidentally kill someone, and it wouldn't be considered murder. We call that *manslaughter*. But this word means "the willful, premeditated killing of an individual out of hatred, anger, desire, or greed."

We all know innately that murder is wrong. Almost every culture throughout the world considers murder a social evil. The Bible contains numerous examples of murder. Way back in the book of Genesis, we read about Cain and Abel, and the first recorded murder. Cain's jealousy led him to murder his own brother Abel. There are many more examples of murder in the Old Testament. Think about King David, the man after God's own heart. After committing adultery with Bathsheba, he sent her husband, Uriah, to the front lines of battle, knowing that he would be killed.

The Old Testament contains several warnings and laws against murder and violence. Proverbs says that God hates "hands that shed innocent blood" (6:17). And the New Testament is replete with examples of murder and violations of the sixth commandment. In fact, Jesus himself was murdered on the cross! But have you ever stopped to ask yourself why murder is wrong? The answer has to do with the character and nature of God.

## DON'T DESTROY GOD'S MASTERPIECE

For the most part, the first four commandments deal with our *vertical* relationship to God—love God first, have no idols, use God's name correctly, and take a Sabbath rest. When we obey and practice the first four commandments, when our vertical relationship with God is good and right, then our *horizontal* relationships will be much healthier. Commandments five through ten deal with the horizontal relationship with others—no murder, no adultery, no stealing, no lying, and no coveting. Both the vertical and the horizontal come into view here within the sixth commandment.

Vertically, we are commanded not to murder because of our relationship with God. Murder damages that relationship. There are two foundational principles at work in the sixth commandment. Both deal with our vertical relationship with God while revealing why the Bible says murder is wrong and why this command was given.

The Bible makes it clear that we are all created in God's image (see Genesis 1:26–28). The word in Hebrew for image is *tzelem,* which means, "something cut out." We were literally made in the image of God; we were "cut out of" Him. We are not God, but we are like God (not bodily, of course) spiritually, intellectually, and morally.

Genesis 9:6 records the following warning from God: "Whoever sheds human blood, by humans shall their blood be shed, for in the image of God has God made mankind." In other words, God declares that murder is wrong because He made us in His image. When we murder another person, we are taking the life of someone also created in God's image. Life is precious to God. Like a great artist, God has put His stamp, His image, and His signature on every one of us. You are loved by God. You are special to God. You are absolutely unique. You are one of a kind. There is no one else like you. To murder is to destroy an original masterpiece of God, someone created in His image.

As the author of life (see Acts 3:14–15), Jesus is the leader, ruler, and prince of all life. In this passage from Acts, the word *life* refers to both physical and spiritual life—both of which belong to Jesus. Life is a gift from Him. As the author of life, God and God alone has the right to give life and to take it away. Therefore, whenever we take another person's life, we are robbing God of His property and His right. When we take someone's life, we take what is not ours and in essence try to become God ourselves. That is what our vertical relationship to God in this commandment is all about.

While there is a vertical responsibility we have to God, there is also a horizontal responsibility to our neighbor. Murder harms the victim and the victim's family, and it ruptures the entire community. It also harms the murderer and his or her extended family. John Calvin expressed it this way: "Our neighbor bears the image of God: To use him, abuse, or misuse him is to do violence to the person of God who images himself in every human soul."

## LIFE AND DEATH ISSUES

This commandment raises a host of hot-button ethical issues: war, capital punishment, abortion, euthanasia, self-defense, and many acts of violence, to name a few. The complexities of these issues go well beyond this short book. However, we can explore a few principles and examples that will guide us through some of the complexities.

Consider the case of war and capital punishment. Recall the definition of murder given earlier—"the willful, premeditated killing of an individual out of hatred, anger, desire, and greed." Notice that the idea of murder here is a personal and individualistic concept. One Bible commentator claims, "This Hebrew verb, *ratsach*, refers only to the killing of a person, never to killing animals, and not even to killing persons in a war. It carries no implications of the means of killing."

War and capital punishment are not being addressed by this command. There are several instances in the Old Testament where war and capital punishment are not only allowed but also commanded by God (see Deuteronomy 20:13, 16–17; 13:5).

These verses don't use the Hebrew word for *murder*. Instead, they use the word for *kill*. In other words, the Bible presents cases where war and capital punishment ultimately promote justice, keep the harmony of the community, and do a greater good.

All of us would agree that stopping Adolf Hitler in World War II was a good thing. He and his armies needed to be stopped and brought to justice for the murder of millions of Jews. Some call this a "just war." The concept of Just War means searching through a number of questions about a particular conflict: Is this war undertaken for a just cause? Does it have a just purpose? Is it carried out with just means? Does a just authority conduct it? Do the benefits outweigh the costs?

When it comes to capital punishment, few of us would want a serial killer stalking freely in our community. Minimally, we want that person behind bars forever. As with war, this is another area where Christians sometimes disagree. Depending on the approach to Scripture, an argument can be made on both sides of the issue. On one hand, the Bible permits and even commands capital punishment. On the other hand, we are told to show grace, mercy, and forgiveness to people. I agree with David W. Gill, professor of ethics at Gordon-Conwell Theological Seminary, who has written:

> It is clear that first-degree murderers deserve to lose their
> life for the one they have taken. The problem we face,

then, is determining how we can justify this severity while excusing ourselves from the harsh penalties prescribed for idolatry, adultery, and so on—of which we are all guilty, given Jesus' explanation of the law. Our calling as Christians in the world is not to make sure people get the punishment they deserve but to bring the good news, hope, and healing in the name of Jesus. Let's direct our energy at ameliorating the conditions and attitudes that lead to capital crimes.[9]

For all of the other difficult life-and-death dilemmas we face—abortion, suicide, killing in self-defense, euthanasia—I rely on a simple biblical principle: Life is sacred and must be protected because we are created in God's image, and He is the author of life. Life is a treasure and a gift from God. We bear His image, and we belong to Him. No matter what the ethical issue is, we need to ask ourselves this question: *Do my attitude and actions reflect the truth that life is sacred and precious to God and thus must be protected, encouraged, and enhanced? In other words, am I a life-giver?*

## THE TRUE LIFE-GIVER

In the Bible the real Life-giver comes onto the scene and turns the world upside down by His life and His message. In the Sermon on the Mount, Jesus takes the sixth commandment and gives it an even deeper and broader meaning:

*You have heard that it was said to the people long ago, "You shall not murder, and anyone who murders will be subject to judgment." But I tell you that anyone who is angry with a brother or sister will be subject to judgment. Again, anyone who says to a brother or sister, "Raca," is answerable to the court. And anyone who says, "You fool!" will be in danger of the fire of hell. (Matthew 5:21–22)*

In these verses Jesus unpacks the true meaning of the sixth commandment. Notice that anger and insults are put in the same category as murder. Murder starts with seething anger and hatred that burns in our hearts and minds, and its final expression can lead to murder. The problem, Jesus says, is our murderous hearts.

As the Sermon on the Mount continues, Jesus says to turn the other cheek (v. 39). Does this mean that we do not protect ourselves in self-defense? Not at all. Self-defense is a way we protect our own lives. What Jesus is saying is that we should not take revenge on those who hurt us. Jesus then makes an outrageous comment: "Love your enemies" (v. 44). He ups the ante even higher when he tells us to "be perfect" (v. 48). Of course, we all know this is impossible—if it's left up to us. But the amazing thing about being a Christian is that we have the power of Christ living in us. It is not a matter of more willpower or positive thinking. No, Jesus in us is the only way we can keep this command.

Jesus was brutally and unfairly murdered on the cross even though He was completely innocent. He was the perfect and guilt-free God-man. Throughout history many people have debated whether it was the Jews or the Romans that murdered Jesus. The correct answer, however, is that we *all* murdered Jesus. Our sins nailed Him to the cross. But the amazing thing here is that Jesus was not a victim. Jesus took upon himself all the penalties as a result of our sin and died in our place. Jesus as the life-giver also means that he opened up the way for us to experience true life, real life, everlasting life. Hebrews 2:10 says, "In bringing many sons and daughters to glory, it was fitting that God, for whom and through whom everything exists, should make the pioneer of their salvation perfect through what he suffered." Jesus made a way of salvation and leads us through it.

## HOPE IN THE CULTURE OF DEATH

How can we promote this idea that life is sacred and must be protected? How do we become life-givers and not life-takers? We can start by watching our speech. Perhaps we have said murderous words to our loved ones—words we wish we could take back. Our words can give life or easily destroy it. From personal experience, I'm very aware that I can harm my loved ones with just a few words. I can also fill them with life with just a few words of love and encouragement.

Second, we need to watch our attitude. Murderous thoughts

of hatred and anger are a real issue for many of us. Of course, some anger is justified. We should be angry about injustice and oppression. We should get angry about sin. When Jesus saw the money changers setting up shop in the courts of the temple, He got angry! The Bible never says that anger is sinful; it's how we handle and deal with anger that leads to sin.

But our anger can also lead to murder. It can crush people's hearts and spirits. It can also destroy their bodies. In his book *Written in Stone*, Philip Graham Ryken provides some practical ways we can move beyond anger by guarding, protecting, and giving life. Ryken writes:

> We can teach our children how to resolve conflict without resorting to violence. We can pray for peace in troubled countries. We can help save children through adoption and foster care. We can care for the sick and the dying. We can send relief to those who are oppressed. We can work to make laws that bring justice and promote life.[10]

In a world of death, suffering, and violence, a world filled with violent images from popular culture, a world of surging anger and hatred, a world that has justly been called "a culture of death," Christians are called to follow Jesus, the author of life. He lived and died to give us life to the full (see John 10:10). So as followers of Jesus, we obey the commandment against murder, and we fulfill Jesus' words to promote life by loving our neighbors in the power of the Holy Spirit.

# 7

# HONORING MARRIAGE AND SEXUALITY

Throughout the Ten Commandments, God doesn't mince words. These commands challenge us to the core of our being. But like a skilled surgeon, God uses His words with careful precision to cut right where the disease lies.

The seventh command is no less painful and personal than the others. As a matter of fact, in some ways it's more painful and more personal than anything we've seen so far: "You shall not commit adultery" (Exodus 20:14). At some level, almost everyone has been affected by the pain of adultery. You might have grown up in a home where this act of betrayal took place, and you still feel the resentment boil up when you think of it. You might be a husband or a wife who discovered your spouse's unfaithfulness, and your whole world fell apart. Perhaps at some point in the recent past you yourself have thought about committing adultery. Or perhaps you've already broken this commandment. No one has to tell you it was wrong; just hearing the word *adultery* fills you again with guilt and shame.

## THREE KINDS OF ADULTERY

Adultery can happen at three different levels. First, and most obviously, there's *physical adultery*. Simply put, physical adultery is voluntary sexual involvement between a married person and someone other than his or her spouse. The primary purpose of the seventh commandment is to protect marriage. This is not talking about sex before marriage, although other parts of the Bible address the sin of sexual union outside the bonds of the biblical marital covenant. This commandment is about breaking the marriage vows through physical, sexual involvement with another person.

There is also what we might call *mental adultery*. This kind of adultery doesn't involve physical intimacy but rather takes place in the mind. Make no mistake: the battle always begins in your mind. Jesus made this point quite clearly when he said, "You have heard that it was said, 'You shall not commit adultery.' But I tell you that anyone who looks at a woman lustfully has already committed adultery with her in his heart" (Matthew 5:27–28).

Jesus wasn't just talking about a single thought or pang of desire. He was referring to what you do with that initial look, thought, or desire. Specifically, Jesus was talking about intentionally and repeatedly indulging in our thoughts and desires. It's when a look becomes a gaze and a gaze becomes an action lived out in your mind. An old saying suggests, "I can't prevent a bird from flying over my head, but I can prevent him from making a nest in my hair."

But please note: this doesn't imply that mental adultery equals physical adultery. Physical adultery breaks the marriage covenant in a way that mental adultery doesn't. Physical adultery is grounds for divorce; mental adultery isn't. Physical adultery defiles one's body, which is the temple of the Holy Spirit, in a way mental adultery doesn't. And physical adultery is something many have avoided, but mental adultery is something no one has totally avoided.

However, mental adultery is so dangerous that Jesus followed up His words about it by saying, "If your right eye causes you to stumble, gouge it out and throw it away. It is better for you to lose one part of your body than for your whole body to be thrown into hell" (Matthew 5:29). Mental adultery may seem harmless to us, but Jesus clearly tells us otherwise.

Finally, there's also *emotional adultery*—developing emotional intimacy with someone other than your spouse. There is a kind of emotional closeness that a married person should share with no one but his or her spouse. Emotional adultery usually begins with a married couple losing that emotional connection they once enjoyed with one another. More and more they become like roommates who live separate lives. A wife no longer feels understood by her husband. A husband feels he can no longer share his true feelings with his wife. When this takes place in a marriage, spouses become vulnerable to this emotional form of adultery. You meet someone, and at first it seems like nothing. You say, "We're just friends. What's wrong with that? He's just someone I do business with." Or, "She understands the pressure I live with. I can talk to her. What's so dangerous about that?"

But a scenario like this often leads to more. Pretty soon you're sharing things you don't share with your spouse. You're keeping meetings and conversations a secret. You find yourself looking forward to seeing that person and spending time with him or her. You're exchanging physical touches that might look platonic to others, but you both know there's more to it than that. This is often how physical adultery starts.

## THE SUPER GLUE OF MARRIAGE

It's no secret that all forms of adultery—physical, mental, or emotional—are rampant today. Some so-called experts even tout the normalcy or even the goodness of adultery. For example, Dr. Catherine Hakim, a sociologist and best-selling British social scientist, argues that a "sour and rigid" view of infidelity condemns millions of people to live frustrated "celibate" lives with their spouses. She likens faithful husbands and wives to "caged animals" and argues that they should be free to explore their "wild side" with lovers without the threat of divorce. In her latest book, *The New Rules*, she calls adulterous flings "parallel relationships." Ms. Hakim claims (quoted in Bingham 2012), "[Adultery] is no more a moral issue than eating a good meal."[11]

Based on this kind of thinking, it's tempting to conclude that adultery isn't really such a big deal after all.

But adultery *is* a big deal because of how God made us as human beings. He made us to be in relationship with Him. This is the thread that runs through the whole Bible: God seeking relationship with people. Throughout the Bible you see Him making covenants with people, and those covenant relationships are defined by commitment and exclusivity. God wants your exclusive loyalty. He alone is your God.

Because we are made in God's image, we are called by God to relate covenantally to other people. For many people that means entering into the covenant of marriage. Usually covenants have signs or seals—something that glues the relationship together. In the New Covenant initiated by Christ, we have the signs of the Lord's Supper—the bread and the cup. God has provided a different sign or seal for the covenant of marriage—the sexual union. Sex was designed by God to be what we might call "covenant cement." It's physical, but it's more than physical. It unites us in body and soul. It binds us together in a way we are bound with no one else. Sex is like Super Glue for the soul: it binds two people together spiritually. But applying Super Glue incorrectly creates a mess. When the wrong things get joined together in matters of the heart, getting them unstuck tears at the soul.

That's why adultery is forbidden. God made us in such a way that sex is a great force for good, but only when used to join one man and one woman for life. Sex is a wondrous and dangerous gift that can either glue a marriage together or tear it apart.

Adultery is also a big deal socially. Marriage is the building block of a healthy society. As marriage goes, so goes a nation. In other words, the world is made up of nations; nations are made up of states; states are made up of cities; cities are made up of communities; communities are made up of families; and families begin with a marriage. According to Michael J. McManus in his article "Why Is it in the Government's Interest To Save Marriages," children of divorce are twice as likely to drop out of school, three times as likely to get pregnant as teenagers, six times as likely to be in poverty, and twelve times more likely to be incarcerated than children whose parents remain married.

Adultery is like an earthquake—the initial event is destructive, but the aftershocks can be more damaging. But even more significant than the social consequences of adultery are the spiritual consequences. Joseph understood this when he told Potiphar's wife, who wanted to start an affair with him, "How then could I do such a wicked thing and sin against God? (Genesis 39:9). David also understood this when he confessed to God after committing adultery with Bathsheba: "Against you, you only, have I sinned and done what is evil in your sight" (Psalm 51:4).

## AN ADULTERY-FREE LIFE

How do we live proactively in the midst of our adultery-happy culture? Here are three actions points that can help you obey this commandment.

*First, work on your relationship with God.* Develop a God-consciousness in which you live in His presence, talk to Him throughout the day, and seek to obey His Word fully. Part of working at your relationship with God involves knowing that you're engaged in a battle. Marriages are under attack; you can't let your guard down. If you think you could never fall into this sin, think again. Not a single follower of Christ is above falling hard in this area. Christians fall. Pastors and church leaders fall. People with good marriages fall. People with bad marriages fall. No one is immune.

In 2 Samuel 11 we see that it was David's ignorance about his own vulnerability that led to his adultery with Bathsheba. David was king of Israel. He had conquered his enemies and established his kingdom. He was living in royal luxury, and he was famous and handsome. His people were at war, but David decided to take it easy. His guard was down. He had stopped serving and giving his life away to others. Sexual sin is never just about sex; it's always connected to the rest of life.

*Second, pursue personal purity in every area of your life.* Listen to Proverbs 4 where a father speaks to his son and gives him godly counsel: "Above all else, guard your heart, for everything you do flows from it" (v. 23). That's where it always starts—in your heart, in your affections, in your mind. And then this father gets practical about how to do this: "Keep your mouth free of perversity; keep corrupt talk far from your lips" (v. 24).

Personal purity starts with the heart, but you have to watch your words as well. We live in a day when many think a filthy mouth is cool. Some believers who have come out of a legalistic background display their freedom in Christ by joking about sexual issues. But Proverbs 4:25 says, "Let your eyes look straight ahead; fix your gaze directly before you." Personal purity starts with your heart, extends to your speech, and then affects what you look at—what you watch on TV, at the movies, on the Internet, at the beach.

Proverbs 4:26–27 says: "Give careful thought to the paths for your feet and be steadfast in all your ways. Do not turn to the right or the left; keep your foot from evil." Personal purity also has to do with where we go. It's like a domino effect. If you don't guard your heart, your mouth will be next, then your eyes, and finally your feet have gone somewhere you never thought they would go.

Personal purity also applies to those who are not married. The discipline and willingness to surrender your will to God's will in this area can make all the difference should you get married. Your fidelity to God now will help you practice fidelity to your spouse later. It may be hard to believe, but sexual temptation is as much a part of the married life as it is a part of the single life. The more you take up your cross now, the better you'll be at it when you get married. So whether you're single or married, pursue personal purity.

*Third, nurture and guard your marriage.* Be intentional about this. Marriage is a wonderful gift full of many joys, but it also involves hard work. If you don't work at it, your marriage will suffer. So be intentional about spending time with your spouse without the kids. Be intentional about communicating openly with each other. Be intentional about serving one another. Be intentional about praying with and for one another. Be intentional about holding one another accountable.

Don't hide anything from your spouse. Secrets destroy a marriage. Your e-mail account should be an open book—websites as well. Movies and TV programs you watch are ones you should be able to enjoy with your spouse present. There are things your spouse and you should agree on as a couple that you will not do with members of the opposite sex. Be intentional about nurturing and guarding your marriage.

## GO AND SIN NO MORE

But what do you do if you've already broken this commandment? You don't have to continue to live in shame and guilt. Nor do you have to stay trapped in the sin of adultery.

In the gospel of John, there's a story about some of the religious leaders who had caught a woman in the act of adultery. They brought her to Jesus and said, "Teacher, this woman was caught in the act of adultery. In the Law Moses commanded us to stone such women. Now what do you say?" (8:4–5). Jesus stooped down and wrote something in the dirt with His finger. We don't know what He wrote, but it reminds us of God himself writing the Ten Commandments on stone tablets with His finger.

What will Jesus say?

He straightened up and said to all of the people who had gathered, "Let any one of you who is without sin be the first to throw a stone at her" (v. 7). One by one they began to leave until Jesus was left alone with the woman. He said, "'Woman, where are they? Has no one condemned you?' 'No one, sir,' she said. 'Then neither do I condemn you,' Jesus declared. 'Go now and leave your life of sin'" (vv. 10–11).

If you can relate to this woman in any way, this passage offers three hopeful truths:

*First, you're not alone.* Every man and woman in that crowd knew they had fallen in the realm of sexuality. If the same challenge were issued today: "Let any one of you who is without sin be the first to throw a stone at her," the room would soon empty.

*Second, forgiveness is possible.* Jesus said, "Then neither do I condemn you." He could say that because He would provide the perfect sacrifice for our sin. Jesus bore the sin of our adultery on the cross so you and I could be freed from its penalty. But to trust Jesus' effective work, you have to bring your sin out in the open. You have to confess it to Him.

*Third, you can change.* Jesus said to the woman, "Go now and leave your life of sin." What a freeing statement! She didn't have to go on living the way she had been. Repentance is a change of mind about sin that causes a change of action toward sin. That's what Jesus means when he says to each one of us, "Go now and leave your life of sin."

# 8

# EXPOSING OUR DECEITFUL HEART

The eighth commandment isn't complicated: "You shall not steal" (Exodus 20:15). *Stealing* can simply be defined as "taking without permission something that doesn't belong to you." That's pretty straightforward, but sometimes we don't realize that we can actually be guilty of stealing a wide variety of things.

## THREE WAYS TO STEAL

*First, we can steal people.* Consider a verse like Deuteronomy 24:7: "If someone is caught kidnapping a fellow Israelite and treating or selling them as a slave, the kidnapper must die." We see how that happened in the story of Joseph. Years after his brothers sold him to the Midianites, he said he was "forcibly carried off from the land of the Hebrews" (Genesis 40:15). Even in our own day, kidnapping is a kind of theft our society punishes severely.

*Second, we can steal physical possessions, including money.* This category includes all conventional types of theft like burglary, robbery, and shoplifting. It also includes white-collar theft like fraud, extortion, embezzlement, and racketeering. I'm certain our economy would be in much better shape if people in high places had listened to the eighth commandment. Five hundred years ago, one pastor identified certain men of his day as "gentlemen swindlers" or "big operators." Some things never change.

There are so many ways we can break the eighth commandment. One prevalent way is by stealing from stores. According to the National Association for Shoplifting Prevention, "There are approximately 27 million shoplifters (or 1 in 11 people) in our nation today. More than 10 million people have been caught shoplifting in the last five years."[12] People also steal from the government. They underpay on their taxes or file false claims for disability. There is also theft at work. Employees help themselves to office supplies, postage stamps, and long-distance phone calls. They pad their expense accounts. According to the U.S. Department of Commerce, employee theft cost businesses over $50 billion annually. The same report estimates that 75 percent of all employees steal at least once and that half of these steal again and again. One of every three business failures is the result of employee theft.[13]

The Internet provides new ways to steal information. Pastors steal sermons, students steal term papers, and businesses steal logos. It seems almost everyone steals music. A Barna Group survey shows that 77 percent of teenagers who consider themselves Christians engaged in at least one type of music piracy in the last six months. And only 10 percent of them believe it's wrong.[14]

By the way, the Old Testament punishment for stealing physical possessions wasn't death but restitution. Not only did you have to pay back what you took but you also had to pay as much as five times the amount. Exodus 22:1 says, "Whoever steals an ox or a sheep and slaughters it or sells it must pay back five head of cattle for the ox and four sheep for the sheep." Can you imagine if we did that today?

*Third, we can steal intangibles.* Jacob stole his brother Esau's blessing when he tricked his father into thinking he was Esau. Interestingly, the Hebrew word for *deceive* literally means, "to steal a person's heart." I can't help but think of how modern politicians have so often stolen the hearts of people, not through hard work and integrity but through empty and deceptive promises.

One of the intangibles that people commonly steal today is a person's good name or reputation through gossip and slander. The severe impact of such theft was seen in the life of the famed nineteenth-century explorer-missionary David Livingstone. In the early days, when he was exploring Africa, he left his wife at home in Great Britain. He wanted to protect her from some of the hardship while he prepared a place for them to live. But back in Britain people began to gossip, saying there was a problem in their marriage. The gossip cut so deep that Livingstone sent for his wife prematurely. After arriving in Africa, she became sick and died. By their slanderous tongues, those people stole from him his reputation, his wife, and his ministry.

## I'VE GOT TO HAVE YOUR STUFF

What drives us to steal? I tried to brainstorm all the reasons people steal, and I came up with a rather large list.

*Some people steal for the thrill of it.* That's what convicted Augustine. He stole a pear from a tree and later said:

> There was a pear tree close to our own vineyard . . . which was not tempting either for its color or for its flavor. Late one night . . . a group of young scoundrels, and I among them, went to shake and rob this tree. We carried off a huge load of pears, not to eat ourselves, but to dump out to the hogs. . . . Doing this pleased us all the more because it was forbidden. Such was my heart, O God. . . . Behold, now let my heart confess to you what it was seeking there . . . having no inducement to evil but the evil itself.[15]

*Some steal because they feel a sense of entitlement.* For some reason, they think they have the right to steal. A few weeks ago, I left my sunglasses at a hotel. I went back and found that no one had turned them in. I'm sure someone found them and said,

"Nice sunglasses. Finders keepers." Or they might have thought, *I'll bet the guy who owned these sunglasses is rich. He probably has three more pairs at home. He won't miss them, and I need them—so it can't hurt if I keep them.* That's entitlement.

*Some people steal because they're lazy.* Why wait for it and work for it when they can get it for free?

*Some steal because they think everyone does it.* They say things like, "Everyone downloads software—why can't I?"

*Some steal because they know they won't get caught.*

*Some steal due to the pervasive greed and selfishness that is a part of our consumer culture.* At times even our leaders urge us to go out and buy stuff. If you don't buy stuff, they say, the system fails. On top of that, advertisers tell us that if we don't buy their products, we won't be attractive or productive. Exodus 20:15 says, "You shall not steal," but if my image, my worth, my productivity, or my very life are supposed to be determined by what I have rather than by what I am, no command against stealing will stop my lust for more things.

## GOD'S RATIONALE FOR "DO NOT STEAL"

Once again we have to ask: If everybody has dozens of reasons for stealing, why does God take such a strong stand against it?

We have to begin with two foundational principles. First, there's the principle of *private property*, which implies that it's legitimate to have possessions. If this were not the case, why would stealing be a problem? God has put us together in such a way that part of our human dignity is wrapped up in acquiring and managing possessions. We understand that God grants us the ability to get wealth and accumulate worldly goods. Thus, when we invade another person's property and steal from him or her, we are sinning against God.

Second, there's the foundational principle of *stewardship*—the idea that everything we have comes from God and ultimately belongs to Him. Someone has said, "In capitalism, the money is yours to do with what you want. In socialism, it belongs to the state, and the state uses it how it wants. In Christianity, it's God's, and it must be used as God directs." Christian author Jerry Bridges says we can have three basic attitudes toward what we have. We can say, "What's yours is mine; I'll take it." That's the attitude of *theft*. We can say, "What's mine is mine; I'll keep it." That's the attitude of *greed*. Or we can say, "What's mine is God's; I'll share it." That's the attitude of *stewardship*.

Sometimes it's our own greed that causes us to cling to our stuff. This greed contributes to creating a society where some people feel they have to steal just to get by. The principle of stewardship says we're called to be generous. In tough economic times, we tend to hold on really tightly to what we have. But are we actually robbing God?

The eighth commandment applies equally to the rich and

the poor, the powerful and the weak. In fact, it was meant to protect the weak against the caprices of the powerful.

Another reason this command is so important is that obeying it builds genuine community. For community to take place, there has to be trust, and trust is impossible in an environment where this commandment is ignored. Instead of trust there is suspicion; instead of acceptance there is resentment; instead of peace there is fear. Anyone who has ever experienced someone breaking into their home and robbing them can tell you about their deep sense of personal violation. It wasn't just that their stuff was taken; something deeper and more precious was violated.

When we break the eighth commandment, what we're really saying is that we can't trust God. Whenever we take something that doesn't belong to us, we're saying that God isn't able to give us everything we truly need. As a matter of fact, when we steal in any of the ways listed above, we're robbing God of the opportunity to supply our needs.

## WE'RE ALL GUILTY THIEVES

When we add together all the ways we can break this commandment, it's easy to see why we don't know anyone who isn't guilty before God. I know I am. It's easy to understand why Martin Luther said, "If we look at mankind in all its conditions, it is nothing but a vast, wide stable of great thieves." So, if none of us is innocent regarding this command, what should we do about it?

We can start by being ruthlessly honest about where we're compromising. It may be something from your past you have never dealt with or something you're involved with right now or something you're thinking about doing in the future. The first thing is to stop rationalizing and call it what it is: sin.

We can go a step further by confessing it as a sin and repenting of it. Confession means agreeing with God about our sin. And part of confession is repentance. Repentance involves a change of *attitude about* sin that causes a change of *action toward* sin. So in order to come fully clean with God, we have to be serious about changing our sinful behaviors.

But it doesn't stop with confession and repentance. If possible, we need to make restitution. We might have to return what we've taken. And if that person, organization, or business we've stolen from has been damaged by our theft beyond the value of what we've taken, we need to find a way to make it up to them. For example, think of Jesus' encounter with Zacchaeus. After Jesus befriended this man who had gotten rich by extorting others, Zacchaeus repented and promised Jesus that he would pay back fourfold anyone he had defrauded.

Finally, we can take a preventive measure against theft: We can learn to practice contentment and gratitude. This is a neglected discipline among believers. How often do you complain about what you don't have? This just ignites an attitude of greed and desire within you. Instead, start practicing gratitude for what you do have, even if you don't feel grateful at first. As you prime the pump of gratitude, you'll find yourself becoming more content, more willing to trust God, more willing to wait on him, more others-centered, and less likely to break this commandment.

## THE THIEF LOVER

It comforts me to know that Jesus died on the cross between two thieves. The Bible says that when Jesus was crucified, "Two robbers were crucified with Him, one on the right and another on the left" (Matthew 27:38 NKJV). This was a fulfillment of the ancient prophecy of Isaiah, who wrote, that Jesus "was numbered with the transgressors" (Isaiah 53:12). Jesus was numbered among thieves so He might suffer and die for our thievery. He died as a thief so that every thief who trusts in Him could be forgiven and saved. The first thief to be saved was hanging right next to Him. He said, "Jesus, remember me when you come into your kingdom" (Luke 23:42). And Jesus promised him what He promises that someday will be true of all of us who trust in Him: "Today you will be with me in paradise" (v. 43).

# 9

# BECOMING TRUTH-LOVERS[16]

In the movie *Liar Liar*, Jim Carrey plays Fletcher Reede, a fast-talking lawyer, habitual liar, and divorced father who built his career on lies. Climbing the corporate ladder has come at the expense of his relationship with his son, Max. Fletcher continuously breaks promises to him. Max, who is disappointed that his dad is missing his birthday party, decides to make a wish. As Max blows out his birthday cake candles, he wishes that his dad could stop lying for twenty-four hours. His wish comes true, and Fletcher's greatest asset, his mouth, becomes his greatest liability—he can only tell the truth.

Fletcher Reede is someone we all can resonate with—because we all lie. But there is an interesting point in the movie that underlines something many of us believe. As Fletcher tries to convince his son to "unwish" the wish, he explains to Max why adults lie: "Sometimes grown-ups need to lie. No one can survive in the adult world if they always had to tell the truth."

If we were honest, deep down, many of us would agree with

that statement. Aren't there times when we need to lie? Little white lies don't hurt anyone, do they? What would our world really be like if we always had to tell the truth? Some people would be out of a job! Consider the following common white lies, and ask yourself if they're really harmless:

The check is in the mail.
You get this one; I'll pay next time.
My wife doesn't understand me.
Trust me, I'll take care of everything.
Of course I love you.
It's not the money; it's the principle of the thing.
But we can still be good friends.
Sure, I'll call you later.
I've never done anything like this.
It wasn't my fault.
I'll pray for you about that.

Have you ever said one of those lies? Are they harmless? Does God really care if we fudge the truth?

## A LIE IS A LIE

The ninth commandment says, "You shall not give false testimony against your neighbor" (Deuteronomy 5:20). To *bear* means to "answer, respond, testify, speak, or shout." *False* is the same Hebrew word used for *vain* in the third commandment—

do not "take the name of the LORD your God in vain" (5:11 NKJV). And *neighbor* does not mean only the people who live next door to us; it refers generically to anyone we come in contact with. Thus, the idea is that we are not to treat or bear witness to our "friend, companion, or fellow" in a vain, empty, and flippant way. Most Bible scholars expand this verse to mean, "Do not lie."

Of course that naturally leads to another question: What is a lie? Here are two definitions:

A lie is "any attempt to distort, shade, or misrepresent the truth."

A lie is "a statement of what is known to be false with intent to deceive."

## LYING ISN'T A VICTIMLESS CRIME

There are three reasons this commandment is so important.

*First, it promotes justice in a court of law.* This commandment, narrowly defined, deals with a courtroom setting. In a courtroom, a witness places his hand on a Bible and promises to "tell the truth, the whole truth, and nothing but the truth, so help [me] God." Truth telling is necessary for justice. Lawyers need both good evidence and trustworthy witnesses to defend or prosecute anyone in the court of law. But justice is impossible without truth. This is true now, and it was true when the commandments were written. In fact, if a witness is found to be a liar, he is to be punished.

According to Deuteronomy 19:15–21, the Bible required two or three witnesses, not just one. But if a witness could not establish a charge made before the authorities and was shown to be a liar, then that witness had to pay the penalty he had sought against the person who was charged with the crime. Notice that the penalty was equal to the charge—life for life, eye for eye, and so on. Being a truthful witness was and still is a serious matter. Here's another challenging verse about the seriousness of truth telling: "If anyone sins because they do not speak up when they hear a public charge to testify regarding something they have seen or learned about, they will be held responsible" (Leviticus 5:1).

In other words, if someone has evidence of a public charge against anyone and withholds that evidence, he "will be held responsible." We call this a sin of omission—not saying or acting in a just matter when you have the power to do so. Promoting and protecting justice in the court of law was the first reason this command was given.

*Second, this commandment protected the communal life of Israel.* Imagine hundreds of thousands of Israelites on the brink of entering the Promised Land. They are tired, beat-up, and weary from their wilderness wanderings. God gives them the Ten Commandments through Moses. Through these commandments they would be able to experience true freedom as God's covenant community. What would happen to this community if they could not trust the court system, the law, or themselves? What if justice, truth, and honesty were the exception and not the rule? Upholding the truth was vital to the community life of Israel. Truth was the foundation they were to build their new lives upon.

The apostle Paul also argued for the necessity of truth telling. In Ephesians 4:25 he writes, "Therefore each of you must put off falsehood and speak truthfully to your neighbor, for we are all members of one body." The word for *falsehood* that Paul used literally means "the lie." Paul says that we are to get rid of the lies and speak the truth because we are members of one another. Because we're members of one body, Paul argues, lying implies hurting others and hurting oneself.

In Colossians 3:9–10, Paul wrote, "Do not lie to each other, since you have taken off your old self with its practices and have put on the new self, which is being renewed in knowledge in the image of its Creator." As followers of Christ we have been given a new set of clothes, a new self. Lying was part of the old self—those stinking, nasty, filthy clothes that we have taken off and thrown away. This new self is being renewed day by day. In both passages Paul's point is clear: falsehood is forbidden in the Christian community. Lying destroys the fabric of the new community under Christ.

*Third, this commandment is rooted in the character and nature of God.* Christians believe that the Bible is the primary way God has chosen to reveal himself to us. God is not hiding from us nor is He elusive. He loves us and desires to give us an abundant life. But God is the one who has set the parameters and guidelines for our life based on his character, and God's nature includes truthfulness. God is called "the God of truth" (Isaiah 65:16 NKJV). Jesus said that He is the way, the truth, and the life (see John 14:6). So God in His essence is truth. He is not *a* truth, but *the* truth. His words are true (see Psalm 119:142, 151), so they can be trusted and followed. Lying is an abomination to Him. Proverbs says that God hates "a lying tongue" and "a false witness who pours out lies" (6:17, 19).

When Jesus was speaking to a group of religious leaders, he said:

> *You belong to your father, the devil, and you want to carry out your father's desires. He was a murderer from the beginning, not holding to the truth, for there is no truth in him. When he lies, he speaks his native language, for he is a liar and the father of lies. (John 8:44)*

According to Jesus, lying borrows from the language of the devil. In fact, the devil is the father of lies. When we lie, we're acting like the devil himself. Honesty is of God; lying is of the devil.

## WHY WE LIE

If lying causes so much damage, why do so many lie? Why does it seem to come so naturally? In 2004, Bella DePaulo, a visiting professor at the University of California, Santa Barbara, and a specialist in studying forms of human deception, asked college students and members of the community-at-large to keep a notebook to tally up the number of lies they told in one week. By the end of the experiment, DePaulo found that the students had lied at least once to 38 percent of the people they came into contact with, while the community-at-large had lied to 30 percent of those with whom they interacted. Based on her research, DePaulo insists that we all fall into one of two categories of liars: We're either "self-centered liars" (we lie in order to make ourselves look better to others) or we're "other-centered liars" (we lie in order to avoid hurting someone else's feelings).

DePaulo's experiment also found that the proverbial "white lie" was more often told to strangers; deeper lies were reserved for those the liar loved most. Here's how DePaulo described these "other-oriented lies":

> [Other-oriented lies] are told for reasons of psychological protection or advantage, but the person protected or advantaged is not the liar. Liars telling other-oriented lies are trying to spare other people from embarrassment, disapproval, conflict, or from getting their feelings hurt.

They also tell such lies in the service of other people's gain or convenience. At least from the liars' point of view, these are kind-hearted, altruistic lies.[17]

There are other ways to explain our penchant for lying. At times we lie because we're afraid. We fear not only the truth but also the consequences that come with the truth. Fear blinds us to the truth. Our lies also stem from pride. We like to act and behave as if we're entirely competent. So when things fall apart, in an attempt to save face, we start scrambling for security—even if that requires a string of lies. Greed can also cause us to lie. In fact, in some respects the major economic crisis of the early twenty-first century stemmed from compounded greed and lies.

## HOW WE LIE

Human beings have developed numerous creative ways to lie. Here's a short list of the major ways.

*False testimony in a court of law* is perhaps the most famous way to break this commandment. A false witness in court (or even out of court) can damage a person's reputation, perpetuating lifelong consequences (i.e., a prison sentence or heavy fines).

*Character assassination* includes *slander* (what we say) and *libel* (what we write) about others that is blatantly dishonest and designed to denigrate someone else. Our media technologies—Facebook, websites, e-mail—have allowed character assassinations to go viral and instantly reach millions of people. Little wonder that an ancient Scripture like Proverbs 10:19 warns us, "When words are many, sin is not absent, but he who holds his tongue is wise" (NIV, 1984).

*Gossip* provides another avenue for breaking the ninth commandment. As someone once said, "Gossip is so nasty that even the word hisses." Gossip is sharing personal or intimate rumors or facts with the intent to be malicious. If you want to destroy a church, just start gossiping about its leaders and people.

*Exaggeration* is another form of lying. We rationalize these "little white lies" by telling ourselves that no one will get hurt.

*Half-truths* consist of statements that are intentionally partially true. Of course, that implies that they also intentionally include untruths. By mixing truth with error we hope to confuse people so they can't detect our deceit. Half-truths involve a subtle "shading" of the truth. For example, let's say someone comes to look at a used car we've put up for sale. When he asks if anything is wrong with the car, we say, "You know, honestly, it has a small oil leak." Technically, that's true, but it's also true that the small oil leak comes from a major engine issue that would cost $2,000 to fix. You've intentionally shaded the truth; you've told a lie.

So how do I lie to you? Let me count the ways. False testimony, slander, libel, gossip, exaggeration, fraud, white lies, and half-truths—all of these modes of lying violate the ninth commandment.

## THE BEAUTY OF TRUTH TELLING

The freedom that God has promised through the Ten Commandments involves a life free from lies. So how do we walk in the truth? How do we unravel the lies in the world and in our own hearts so we can enjoy the goodness of truth?

First, we need to pursue the truth with passion. The Russian novelist, essayist, and Gulag (forced labor camps of the Soviet Union) survivor Alexander Solzhenitsyn died on August 3, 2008, at age eighty-nine. About thirty years prior to his death, Solzhenitsyn offered his wisdom to the 1978 graduating class of Harvard University. In a speech filled with memorable, challenging, and even shocking quotes, Solzhenitsyn had offered this way of pursuing truth:

> Harvard's motto is "Veritas" [Latin for truth]. Many of you have already found out, and others will find out in the course of their lives, that truth eludes us if we do not concentrate with total attention on its pursuit. And even while it eludes us, the illusion still lingers of knowing it and leads to many misunderstandings. Also, truth is seldom pleasant; it is almost invariably bitter.[18]

Truth is an elusive concept that is misunderstood by many

today. We live in a culture that often parrots this all-too-familiar mantra of postmodernism: "What's true for you is your truth, and what's true for me is my truth. Whatever you do, just don't push your truth on me!" But for the follower of Christ, truth exists because truth is intimately connected with a person—Jesus Christ. Truth is not some abstract idea; it's an attribute of God. Because God is Truth, He can be trusted. Jesus claimed to be truth personified (see John 14:6 and Ephesians 4:21). Jesus' words are true and faithful. The Holy Spirit leads us into the truth (see John 16:13). The Bible teaches us to know truth (see John 8:32), to do the truth (see John 3:21), and to abide in the truth (see John 8:44). Our position in Christ rests in the truth (see James 1:18). Truth is found in God's Word, the Bible, and must be obeyed (see Romans 2:8; Galatians 5:7). Truth exists, but we must make a commitment to pursue the living truth found in Jesus and His Word.

As followers of Christ we also need to practice speaking the truth in love. The apostle Paul wrote, "Instead, speaking the truth in love, we will grow to become in every respect the mature body of him who is the head, that is, Christ" (Ephesians 4:15). Part of being a mature believer involves learning to speak the truth in love. Why? So we can grow up in every way into Christ, the head of the church. By speaking and doing the truth in love, we mature in the faith and proportionally become more like Christ.

However, speaking the truth doesn't give us a license to say whatever is on our mind. It is possible to speak the truth in a sinful and arrogant way. We're explicitly told to speak the truth *in love*. Paul urged us to speak gracious words, words that are "seasoned with salt" (see Colossians 4:6).

Finally, as we pursue truth and speak the truth in love, we can also practice simple honesty in our speech. One of the ways to practice simple honesty is to be willing to say, "I was wrong. I made a mistake." We can only wonder how history would have changed if that were the American way. After Watergate, Richard Nixon might have fired a handful of misguided supporters, apologized to the public, and turned over the evidence to a prosecutor. Honesty may have saved his presidency. Bill Clinton could have immediately admitted he did have sex with that woman, apologized, and that may have been the end of it. George W. Bush could have reported immediately that Karl Rove had leaked the CIA agent's name and punished him appropriately. It could have been over. Simple honesty in these three cases would have saved the American people hundreds of millions of tax dollars spent on investigations and some of the most embarrassing pages ever written in U.S. history books.

## HOPE FOR RECOVERING LIARS

Maybe there is someone you need to have an honest conversation with so you can come clean in that relationship. Maybe a lie has been weighing you down—perhaps you're even drowning in it—and you need to let it out.

Several years ago, while I was still a seminary student, I lied to one of my professors. I told him I had completed a reading assignment that I had not finished. Since our grade was based on the honor system, I received a decent grade based on the belief that I had completed the assigned reading. Years later, when I was serving on the pastoral staff of a church, the Lord convicted me of the need to come clean with my professor. I wrote him a letter, confessing my lie and seeking to make it right in whatever way possible. I waited anxiously for his reply, knowing that he had every right to revoke my degree. About two weeks later I received the following gracious letter:

Dear Mark,

Thank you for your good letter. I value deeply your willingness to acknowledge the failure to list your reading accurately for the course. The pressure to ratify course requirements can be tempting.

But through this you have received grace to acknowledge this. Calvin said that true and lasting repentance follows our union with Christ through grace. I accept your confession as a sign of God's grace in your life—and you should, too!

God bless you in your continued ministry and study.

Now read the book because you want to, not because you have to!

Cordially,

Ray S. Andersen

Needless to say, God used Dr. Anderson to show me His amazing grace in a whole new way. The fact is that we're all guilty of some form of lying. The answer isn't in just trying to be good, truth-telling men and women. No, we are called to put our faith and our lives into the hands of the only person who never uttered a single lie—Jesus Christ. When we do that, not only will He forgive us, but also His grace will compel us to love the truth and to become truth-tellers in all we do.

# FACING OUR
# COVETOUS HEART

Thomas J. DeLong, a professor at Harvard Business School, has noted a disturbing trend among his students and colleagues. He calls it a "comparison obsession." DeLong writes:

A former student of mine who graduated ten years ago and has a terrific job at a Fortune 500 company still suffers from this comparison obsession. At least it seemed like a terrific job until she received her alumni newsletter and learned that a fellow alumnus, who was in the MBA program with her, had just been named VP at a Fortune 100 company. From that moment on, she could barely hold a conversation without bemoaning her lack of VP and Fortune 100 company status; on more than one occasion, she told others she felt like a failure.

More so than ever before . . . [the people I meet] are obsessed with comparing their own achievements against those of others. Over the last five years, I have . . .

discovered that comparing has reached almost epidemic proportions. . . . It's telling that in my 500 interviews of "high-need-to-achieve-professionals" over the past three years, more than 400 of them questioned their own success and brought up the name of at least one other peer who they felt had been more successful than they were. Many of these individuals are considered among the best and the brightest, yet they are trapped by their comparing reflex.[19]

There's another word for DeLong's observations about wanting what someone else has—it's called *covetousness*. Of course God warned us about this problem a long time ago. The tenth commandment is very clear about wanting what others have: "You shall not covet your neighbor's house. You shall not covet your neighbor's wife, or his male or female servant, his ox or donkey, or anything that belongs to your neighbor" (Exodus 20:17).

But here's the odd truth about this commandment: we just don't think about it very much. After all, it's the last one on the list. But as we'll explore later in this chapter, of all the commandments, the apostle Paul admitted that this one was the hardest to observe. How do we control covetousness? Is it even possible to conquer it?

## I WANT IT RIGHT NOW!

What is covetousness, anyway? Interestingly, unlike murder, covetousness isn't a behavior. It's not something we do. Covetousness is much more like a feeling, or a deep wanting. To covet is to crave, to yearn for something, to hanker after something that belongs to someone else. According to the tenth commandment, coveting encompasses setting our hearts on anything that's not rightfully ours. Coveting is the sin of desire. You see something, it's not yours, but you want it anyway—no, you *crave* it; your heart *demands* it right now.

Not all desires are bad, of course. God made us as creatures of desire. Our desire for food reminds us to eat. Our desire to do something useful motivates us to work. Our desire for friendship draws us into community. And the greatest of all desires is the desire to know God and please Him. Coveting isn't just about desiring bad things, though. It usually involves desiring good things in a bad way.

In other words, coveting always entails some kind of twisted, deformed, demanding desire for what is not rightfully ours. Coveting is why you focus on what you don't have instead of being grateful for what you do have. Coveting is what causes that little twinge of disappointment when someone else gets something you want. It's how you react when a co-worker gets the promotion, when your roommate finds romance, when your friend goes on a dream vacation, or when your neighbors get a new addition to their house—and you don't. You can even covet spiritual experiences: *Why does she have an amazing prayer life and I don't? Why does he feel so close to God, and I seldom have powerful experiences of God's presence?* As the text from Deuteronomy seems to imply with its long list of what not to covet, almost anything good and decent can become an opportunity for covetousness.

## IT'S WORSE THAN YOU THINK

The tentacles of covetousness reach deep into the human heart. We'd like to assume that breaking the tenth commandment pales in comparison to the other commandments. After all, isn't coveting just a "little sin"? We'd also like to think that covetousness is an easy foe to conquer: Just use a little will power and maybe throw in a little religious prayer and *poof!*—coveting has been quickly eliminated from the depths of our heart.

But the apostle Paul knew the lure of our sinful heart much better than that. Paul was committed to the Ten Commandments. He ordered his life around them. But "do not covet" posed a real challenge for him.

To understand the depths of Paul's life-and-death battle with covetousness, we have to understand his life story. Paul was born a long way from Jerusalem in a place called Tarsus. That's in the southern part of what we call Turkey. He was circumcised on the eighth day, which means he was born into the Jewish faith. He wasn't circumcised as an adult convert; he was an insider from the start. Not only that but he was also a descendent of the tribe of Benjamin, one of the most respected tribes in all Israel. Benjamin was special; he was the only one of Jacob's twelve children to be born in the Promised Land. Benjamin's warriors were famous for their bravery. Paul was named after Israel's first king, Saul, who came from the tribe of Benjamin. Jerusalem, the holy city, was in Benjamin's territory.

Paul was a Hebrew of Hebrews, born into the faith, and descended from the tribe of Benjamin. But that's not all. He began to learn the law of God in his fifth year. When he was ten, he began studying to become a Pharisee, a select group of men with a long tradition of zealous adherence to the law. When he was thirteen, he was sent to Jerusalem to study under Gamaliel, the best scholar of his day. In Paul's day that was the equivalent of getting an advanced degree from Harvard. Even among the Pharisees, nobody was more committed than Saul. He was passionate about preserving his Jewish heritage. That's why he went after the new followers of Jesus. Christianity was a threat to his ancient faith, and he did everything he could to rid the world of those heretics.

But there came a time when the things he learned collided with his own sinfulness. Paul's heart became a warzone, and the greatest battle he faced involved the sin of covetousness. For

Paul, this is the one sin that tripped him up. Here's how Paul described his battle with coveting in Romans 7:7–8:

*What shall we say, then? Is the law sinful? Certainly not! Nevertheless, I would not have known what sin was had it not been for the law. For I would not have known what coveting really was if the law had not said, "You shall not covet." But sin, seizing the opportunity afforded by the commandment, produced in me every kind of coveting. For apart from the law, sin was dead.*

Coveting wasn't just Paul's worst battle; it was his biggest defeat. It was the sin that got him.

The tenth commandment exposed a different kind of desire in Paul's heart. It was like something good had been twisted. He was never satisfied, never content. He began to see that his desire did not include love of God or of men. If he truly loved God, he should have been utterly content and grateful for what He gave him. But he wanted more. It wasn't material things he desired. It was ambition. It was the drive to surpass others in everything he did. And he could never get enough—enough attention, enough acclaim, enough recognition. He didn't love God, nor did he love other people. He loved himself above everything else. He knew this because whenever he got what he wanted, he didn't rejoice. He may have feigned happiness, but deep down he seethed; he envied.

## THE CRUELEST CAPTOR

The tenth commandment exposed the power of sin in Paul's life. When it came to coveting, Paul discovered that coveting isn't like giving in to a bad habit that you can stop at any time. No, for Paul, coveting was much more like being enslaved by a cruel captor.

Do you remember Gollum from Tolkien's Lord of the Rings trilogy? Gollum is the slimiest, wiliest, and most pathetic creature in the entire series. But before he became Gollum, he was a normal and perhaps even happy Hobbit named Smeagol. Tragically, Smeagol became obsessed with one dark desire—to own and use the Ring. By coveting the Ring, Smeagol-Gollum still vaguely recalled good gifts like friendship and love, but deformed desires had captured his heart. They were the desires of a dark and sinister wanting for something that was not his.

In a conversation between Gandalf and Frodo Baggins, here's how Tolkien described the cruel chains of covetousness:

> [Gandalf said], "There was nothing more to find out, nothing worth doing, only nasty furtive eating and resentful remembering. [Gollum] was altogether wretched. He hated the dark, and he hated light more: he hated everything, and the Ring most of all.
>
> "What do you mean?" said Frodo. "Surely the Ring was his precious and the only thing he cared for? But if he hated it, why didn't he get rid of it, or go away and leave it?"

"You ought to begin to understand, Frodo, after all you have heard," said Gandalf. "He hated it and loved it, as he hated and loved himself. He could not get rid of it. He had no will left in the matter."[20]

The tenth commandment is last not because it is least but because it is the root of everything else. Why do people steal? Why do people murder? Why do they commit adultery? It's because desire has become twisted and is out of control. This is where sin always starts. First, we want something. Then we start thinking about how much we want it. Soon it starts to dominate our thoughts until finally it becomes an obsession. When we get to that point, sin will have its way with us. Before we know it, we've even broken the first commandment. That thing we covet has become for us a god.

Paul began to realize that God wanted more from him than just keeping the rules. He wanted Paul's heart. He wanted to penetrate beneath the surface of his life. He wanted inward righteousness as well as outward obedience.

## THE SECRET ANTIDOTE

During Paul's dramatic encounter with the risen Christ on the road to Damascus, when that blinding light knocked him to the ground, he was already struggling. Deep down he knew he had not just broken the tenth commandment, but all of them.

When Paul heard the voice of Jesus, he knew he needed the salvation Jesus offered. Despite his impeccable background and pedigree, despite his incredible track record and religious resume, Paul needed forgiveness and freedom as much as anybody else. Paul put his faith in Jesus Christ and began to learn of what he would later call "the boundless riches of Christ" (Ephesians 3:8).

Little by little, Paul began to learn the secret of contentment: Jesus is enough. This is the lesson we all must learn in the winning the battle with our covetous hearts. Contentment starts from within. It starts with knowing God, who loved us enough to send His Son for us. It starts with trusting that He will meet all our needs. When you know Christ and allow His life to well up within you, He gradually begins to reorder your disordered desires. You begin to want what He wants for you. As Christ fills and satisfies your heart, you can rejoice in whatever He chooses to give to others as well. In Paul's words, you can start to "rejoice with those who rejoice" (Romans 12:15).

When Paul wrote to the Philippians, he shared the secret to winning the battle against covetousness: finding contentment in Christ. Paul put it this way in Philippians 4:11–13:

*I have learned to be content whatever the circumstances. I know what it is to be in need, and I know what it is to have plenty. I have learned the secret of being content in any and every situation, whether well fed or hungry, whether living in plenty or in want. I can do all this through him who gives me strength.*

The secret is Christ—the risen Christ at work in your heart, filling you up and giving you the strength to trust Him. Circumstances, people, and recognition do not make you content; only Jesus can give the true contentment that liberates you from the bondage of covetousness. When you have Christ, when you rest in who He is and what He provides, you have enough. You have in your possession those "boundless riches of Christ" (Ephesians 3:8). With all of that, why would you covet anything?

# CONCLUSION

As those who have embraced the gospel of grace, we don't ignore God's law; rather, we gladly embrace it. Not only do we want to please the One who rescued us but we also know that this is the path to true freedom.

Dorothy Sayers, the mystery writer, was a devoted Christian. In trying to explain the value of God's law, she pointed out that in our society there are two kinds of laws. There is the *law of the stop sign*, and there's the *law of the fire*. The law of the stop sign is a law that says the traffic is heavy on a certain street, and as a result the police department or the city council decides to erect a stop sign. They also decide that if you run that stop sign, it will cost you $25 or $30 or $35. If the traffic changes, they can up the ante. That is, if too many people are running the stop sign, they can make the fine $50 or $75, or if they build a highway around the city, they can take the stop sign down, or reduce the penalty, making it only $10 if you go through. The police department or city council controls the law of the stop sign.

But the law of the fire says that if you put your hand in the fire, you will get burned. Now imagine that all of the legislatures of all the nations of the entire world gathered in one great assembly, and they voted unanimously that fire would no longer burn.

The first man or woman who left that assembly and put his or her hand in the fire would discover that the law of the fire is different from the law of the stop sign. Bound up in the nature of fire itself is the penalty for abusing it. So, Sayers explains, the law of God as revealed in the Ten Commandments is like the law of the fire. You never break God's laws; you just break yourself on them. God can't reduce the penalty, because the penalty for breaking the law is bound up in the law itself.

As followers of Jesus Christ, we know that He paid the ultimate penalty for our neglect and failure to keep God's law, but we also know that He is in the process of transforming us into people who love His law and keep His law. He does this not to restrict us but to free us from the penalty bound up in the law itself.

# NOTES

1. John Calvin, Calvin's Bible Commentary: Harmony of the Law Part 2 (Charleston: Forgotten Books, 2007), 127.

2. With special thanks to Justin Buzzard for his sermon titled "The Name" preached at Central Peninsula Church on February 1, 2009.

3. Quoted in Associated Press, "Joe Paterno Distraught after Firing," ESPN .com, August 15, 2012, http://espn.go.com/college-football/story/_/ id/8272847/penn-state-nittany-lions-joe-paterno-distraught-firing.

4. Stephen L. Carter, God's Name in Vain (New York: Basic Books, 2001), 16.

5. Ted Koppel, "The Vannatizing of America," DUKE Magazine, July/ August 1987, 36.

6. Barbara Brown Taylor, "Divine Subtraction," Christian Century, November 3, 1999.

7. Eugene Peterson, "The Pastor's Sabbath," Leadership Journal, Spring 1985.

8. With special thanks to Rob Hall for his sermon titled "Life Is Sacred" preached at Central Peninsula Church on March 22, 2009.

9. David W. Gill, Doing Right (Downers Grove: IVP Press, 2004), 197.

10. Philip Graham Ryken, Written in Stone (Phillipsburg: P&R Publishing, 2010), 144.

11. John Bingham, "Puritan View of Adultery Turns Brits into 'Caged Animals' Says Academic" The Telegraph, August 20, 2012.

12. Information and statistics provided by the National Association for Shoplifting Prevention (NASP), a nonprofit organization that shapes,

promotes, and supports comprehensive community action in shoplifting prevention efforts. Contact NASP at 800-848-9595 or visit www.shopliftingprevention.org.

13. Mary Goodman and Rich Russkoff, "Employee Theft: Are You Blind to It?" *CBS News*, July 14, 2011.

14. Barna Group, "Fewer Than 1 in 10 Teenagers Believe that Music Piracy Is Morally Wrong," April 26, 2004.

15. Augustine, *Confessions* (New York: Oxford University Press, 2009), 29.

16. With special thanks to Rob Hall for his sermon titled "Liar, Liar" preached at Central Peninsula Church on February 22, 2009.

17. Bella DePaulo, "The Many Faces of Lies," last accessed on August 27, 2012, http://smg.media.mit.edu/library/DePaulo.ManyFacesOfLies.pdf.

18. Alexander Solzhenitsyn, *A World Split Apart* (New York: Harper Collins, 1978), 1.

19. Thomas J. DeLong, "Why Chronic Comparing Spells Career Poison," *CNN Money*, June 20, 2011.

20. J. R. R. Tolkien, *The Fellowship of the Ring* (New York: Mariner Press, 2005), 60.

# NOTE TO THE READER

The publisher invites you to share your response to the message of this book by writing Discovery House, P.O. Box 3566, Grand Rapids, MI 49501, U.S.A. For information about other Discovery House books, music, or DVDs, contact us at the same address or call 1-800-653-8333. Find us at dhp.org or send e-mail to books@dhp.org.